CHAMPIONS OF THE QUEEN

40 glorious years of sport

A celebration compiled by
DAVID HUNN

Granta Editions
in association with
The Central Council of
Physical Recreation

Foreword

THE concept of the Queen's champion goes back to the days of chivalry in Medieval times. The knight or warrior would represent his monarch in battle or tournament. He would carry the Queen's favour. His victory would be her victory, and his honour would be her honour. Out of this custom grew the tradition that the knight was never fighting for his sake alone; he fought for a cause that went beyond himself.

That proud custom lives on, transmitted into the tradition of the sporting champion. Every champion, it is true, struggles to gain personal success for him or herself, but what gives a world championship its essential character is its international dimension. The participants are representing their own country. Every nation understandably thrills to the success of its own sporting heroes and heroines. This is not cheap chauvinism; it is the admiration of excellence, the recognition of creative endeavour at its highest, the acknowledgement of what skill allied to dedication can achieve. It creates a desire in the young to emulate the deeds of their champions. At its best, sport has an enormous capacity for social good. It inspires the participant and the spectator alike. No public activity offers such a shared experience or binds a nation so closely together as its sport. In saluting our champions we are paying tribute to the better part of ourselves.

Every sporting organisation that has a member of the royal family as its President or Patron knows the immense value of this association. The Queen and her family are no mere figureheads. Their interest in sport is deep and abiding.

Moreover, they are themselves truly royal champions. Prince Philip is the only President of an International Sports Federation to be a world champion in his own right. The Princess Royal is an Olympic equestrian medallist. Her Presidency of the British Olympic Association and Prince Philip's Presidency of the CCPR and the British Sports Trust are two examples among many of how the concept of champion has come full circle. Their Royal Highnesses now champion the cause of sport.

It is this identification of royalty with their champions, and of their champions with the people, that is so uplifting in a democratic age. Sport knows no barriers. Sport is for all.

How fitting it is, therefore, that we should be celebrating forty years of Her Majesty's reign by honouring again, within this CCPR publication, those many British world champions who, since 1952, have inspired us by their extraordinary feats and reawakened the echoes of chivalric, heroic deeds.

PETER LAWSON
General Secretary, CCPR

DAVID HUNN, author and editor of 'Champions of the Queen', has reported on more than 100 different sports – almost certainly more than anyone else in the world – has written ten books and in 1992 covers his sixth Olympic Games. He wrote for The Observer for 22 years and after moving to the Sunday Times won the 1991 Doug Gardner Memorial Award for his outstanding contribution to sports journalism.

Picture research by Alan Road.

Cover: Press Association (Roger Bannister, Henry Cooper, Ian Botham), Syndication International (Virginia Wade).

Back Cover: Sport & General.

H.M. The Queen: Press Association, Associated Press.

Sports pictures (colour): AllSport Photographic, Associated Press, Colorsport.

Sports pictures (black and white): Sport & General, **Press Association,** Ed Lacey/.A.S.P., Hulton Pictures, The Observer.

© The Central Council of Physical Recreation, 1992

ISBN 0 906782 89 9

Published by Granta Editions, 47 Norfolk Street, Cambridge CB1 2LE,
in association with
The Central Council of Physical Recreation.

All right reserved. No part of this publication may be reproduced, stored in any retrieval system or transmitted in any form or by any means, electronic, mechanical, photocopying, recording or otherwise, without prior written permission of the copyright holder for which application should be addressed in the first instance to the publishers. No liability shall attach to the authors, the copyright holder or the publishers for loss or damage of any nature suffered as a result of reliance on the reproduction of any of the contents of this publication or any errors or omissions in its contents.

Jacket design by Tony Mullins
Book designed by Peter Dolton.

Design and production in association with
Book Production Consultants,
47 Norfolk Street, Cambridge CB1 2LE.

Printed and bound by
Foister & Jagg, Abbey Walk, Cambridge.

BUCKINGHAM PALACE.

Anyone involved in international sport has to be forward-looking. It's always the next championships or the next Olympic Games that provide the challenge and the opportunity to win success and fame. Yet success is built on success. Where others have led the way in developing techniques in training and preparation and setting records, their followers build on their experience and are challenged to do better still.

The last time the Olympic Games were held in this country was in 1948, just after the war ended and only four years before the Queen came to the throne. Since then forty years have slipped past and with them have gone some great sporting occasions and achievements. This book is not pure nostalgia, it is a valuable record of the outstanding international sporting successes of British men and women during the Queen's reign.

Many of the individual champions and members of winning teams became national heroes and have remained heroes within their own sports. Others have packed away their spikes or boots and gone off to pursue careers in other fields. They are all included in this book and I hope that their example will encourage the younger readers to see that talent, hard work and dedication can bring spectacular success.

1992

BRITAIN'S WORLD AND OLYMPIC CHAMPIONS 1952-91

The year noted is that in which an individual championship was won.
Turn to that year to find its details. The list is not absolutely definitive: for instance,
none of the very large number of British world champions in the various classes
of sailing have been included.

ACLAND, Janet **1988**
ADAMS, Neil **1981**
AITKEN-WALKER, Louise **1990**
ALEXANDER, Steve **1981**
ALLAN, Alister **1978**
ALLCOCK, Tony **1986-87-89-90-91**
ALLEN, Katrina **1987**
ALTWEGG, Jeanette **1952**
ANDERSON, Bob **1988**
ANDERSON, Fergus **1953-54**
ANDRIES, Dennis **1986-89-90**
ANGUS, Howard **1973-76-77-79**
ASHURST, Kevin **1982**
ATKINS, Geoffrey **1954-63-64-67-70**
ATKINSON, Jerome **1984**
AUGLE, Myrtle **1988**

BAILLIEU, Chris **1977**
BARRON, Jonathan **1970**
BASS, Rita **1986**
BEDFORD, David **1971**
BEETHAM, Herbert **1960**
BELL, Derek **1985**
BELL, Diane **1985-86-87**
BETTS, Terry **1972**
BHAIRO, Nahrinda **1981**
BIDWELL, John **1988**
BODEN, Peter **1991**
BOONE, Willie **1984-85**
BOUGARD, Fleur **1990**
BRAITHWAITE, Bob **1968**
BRANSON, Clive **1987**
BRASHER, Chris **1956**
BRIDGE, Jane **1980**
BRIGGS, Karen **1982-84-86-89**
BRISTOW, Eric **1980-81-84-85-86**
BROOME, David **1970**
BRUNDLE, Martin **1988**
BRYANT, David **1966-79-80-81-86-87-88-89-90-91**
BUCHANAN, Ken **1970**
BUDD, Zola **1985-86**
BURTON, Beryl **1959-60-62-63-66-67**

CALDWELL, David **1985**
CARTER, Kenny **1983**
CHARLES, Vic **1986**
CHURCHILL, John **1978**
CLARK, Jim **1963-65**
CLARK, Lin **1985**
CLOKE, Chris **1985**
COAKES, Marion **1965**
COE, Sebastian **1980-84**
COLCLOUGH, Brian **1962-65**
COLCLOUGH, Patricia **1962-65**
COLLINS, Jim **1984**
COLLINS, Peter **1976-77-80-83-84**

COLLINS, Ronald **1972-73-74-75-76-77-78-79**
CONTEH, John **1974**
COOPER, Malcolm **1978-82-83-84-86-88-90**
COOPER, Patricia **1958**
COOPER, Sydney **1958**
CORSIE, Richard **1989-91**
COUSINS, Robin **1980**
COWLER, Gerry **1984**
CRAM, Steve **1983**
CRAVEN, Peter **1955-62**
CROCKFORD, Beryl **1985**
CURRY, John **1976**
CURTIS, Steve **1987**

DAGLEY, Norman **1971-75-87**
DAVIES, Chris **1972**
DAVIES, Lynn **1964**
DAVIES, Susan **1990**
DAVIS, Fred **1952-53-54-55-56-80-81**
DAVIS, Steve **1981-83-84-87-89**
DEAN, Christopher **1981-82-83-84**
DEAR, James **1955**
DELLER, Keith **1983**
DEMMY, Lawrence **1952-53-54-55**
DENNY, Doreen **1959-60**
DIXON, Robin **1964-65**
DOWNES, Terry **1961**
DOYLE, Loretta **1982**
DOYLE, Tony **1980-86**
DRIFFIELD, Leslie **1967-71**
DUFF, Hugh **1988**
DUKE, Geoff **1952-53-54-55**

EDMONDS, Ray **1972-74-85**
ELDON, Stan **1958**
ELLIS, Ted **1952**
EMUS, Alan **1961-65-69**
EVANS, Mal **1972**
EYRE, Denise **1984**

FALDO, Nick **1989**
FARRANT, Paul **1959**
FELLOWS, Penny **1989**
FIELDING, Barbara **1971**
FINNEGAN, Chris **1968**
FIORE, Peter **1978**
FISHER, Alison **1985**
FLETCHER, Roger **1988**
FOGARTY, Carl **1989**
FOLLEY, John **1969**
FORD, Bernard **1966-67-68-69**
FOSTER, Frank **1956**
FOWLER, Roy **1963**

FOX, Richard **1981-83-85-89**
FULFORD, Robert **1990**
FULLERTON, Terry **1973**
FURRER, Carl **1980-82**
GARSIDE, Alex **1989**
GILL, Kevin **1986**
GOODHART, Nick **1956**
GOODHEW, Duncan **1980**
GORDON-WATSON, Mary **1970**
GOULD, Rod **1970**
GRANT, Sally **1989**
GREEN, Lucinda **1982**
GREGORY, Paul **1983**
GRIFFITHS, Terry **1979**
GRINHAM, Judy **1956**

HAILWOOD, Mike **1961-62-63-64-65-66-67-78**
HARRIS, Reg **1952-54**
HARRIS, Robin **1969**
HART, Michael **1977**
HASLAM, Ron **1979**
HAWTHORN, Mike **1958**
HAZELWOOD, Mike **1977-79-81**
HEAPS, Ian **1975**
HEATLEY, Basil **1961**
HEMERY, David **1968**
HENDRY, Stephen **1990**
HIGGINS, Alex **1972-82**
HILL, Graham **1962-68**
HILL, John **1980-81-84-85**
HILLYARD, Stacey **1984**
HILLYER, Anthea **1980-82-83-86-90**
HINES, Martin **1983-91**
HOBBS, Elizabeth **1983-84**
HODGE, Sally **1988**
HOLMES, Andrew **1987-88**
HONEYGHAN, Lloyd **1986-87-88**
HOPE, Maurice **1979**
HOSKYNS, Bill **1958**
HUGHES, Ann **1986**
HUGHES, Robert **1972**
HUNT, James **1976**

IVY, Bill **1967**

JAY, Allan **1959**
JENKINS, Roger **1982**
JESSUP, David **1980**
JOHNSON, Albert **1957**
JONES, Courtney **1957-58-59-60**
JONES, Jonathan **1986-89**
JONES, Mandy **1982**
JORDAN, Paul **1976**

KARNEHM, Jack **1969**
KELLY, Danny **1963**
KENNETT, Gordon **1978**
KERR, Albert **1977**

LANE, William **1963**
LAWTON, Duncan **1981**
LEADBETTER, Brian **1987-91**
LEDEN, Judy **1987-91**
LEE, George **1976-78-81**
LEE, Michael **1980-81**
LE MOIGNAN, Martine **1989**
LENG, Virginia **1986**
LOMAS, Bill **1955-56**
LONSBROUGH, Anita **1960**
LOUIS, John **1976**
LOWE, John **1979-87**
LUXON, Paul **1972**
LYLE, Sandy **1988**

McCAULEY, Dave **1989**
McCOLGAN, Liz **1991**
McCRORY, Glenn **1989**
McDONALD, Kirsty **1984**
McDONALD-SMITH, Iain **1968**
McGOWAN, Walter **1966**
McGUIGAN, Barry **1985**
McKAY, Patrick **1982-84**
McKENZIE, Duke **1988-91**
McTAGGART, Richard **1956**
MAGRI, Charlie **1983**
MALE, James **1988-90**
MAPPLE, Andy **1981**
MARKHAM, June **1957-58**
MARSH, Terry **1987**
MARTIN, Louis **1959-62-63-65**
MATTHEWS, Ken **1964**
MATTHEWS, Roy **1955**
MATTHEWS, Stewart **1980**
MEADE, Richard **1972**
MERCER, Marion **1952**
MEREDITH-HARDY, Richard **1990**
MICHAEL, Barry **1985**
MINTER, Alan **1980**
MOORE, Stephen **1988**
MOORHOUSE, Adrian **1988**
MORGAN, Darren **1987**
MORTON, Chris **1984**
MOUNTJOY, Doug **1976**

NADIN, Simon **1989**
NASH, Tony **1964-65**
NEIGHBOUR, John **1987-89**
NICKS, Jennifer **1953**
NICKS, John **1953**
NORMAN, Wendy **1982**
NORRIS, Fred **1959**
NOYCE, Graham **1979**
NUDD, Robert **1990-91**

OAKES, Judy **1981-82-88**
O'DELL, George **1977**
OLIVER, Eric **1953**
O'REILLY, Wilfred **1991**
OSBORN, John **1976**

OVETT, Steve **1980**
OWEN, Gary **1963-66**

PACKER, Ann **1964**
PARROTT, John **1991**
PARROTT, Tim **1989-90**
PARSONS, Terry **1982**
PATTISSON, Rodney **1968-72**
PAWSON, John **1988**
PAWSON, Tony **1984**
PEACOCK, Cyril **1954**
PEARCE, Shaun **1991**
PENDRY, John **1985**
PENGELLY, Edward **1976-77-78-79-81-85**
PEPPER, Jacqueline **1987**
PERRY, Nora **1980-83**
PETERS, Mary **1972**
PICKERING, Thomas **1989**
PINSENT, Matthew **1991**
POND, David **1967**
PORTER, Hugh **1968-70-72**
POTTER, Martin **1989**
PRENN, John **1981-82-83-86-87-90**
PRESSLEY, James **1991**
PRICE, John **1990**
PRICE, Mary **1991**
PRIESTLEY, Dennis **1991**
PULMAN, John **1957-64-65-66-68**

RAND, Mary **1964**
READ, Phil **1964-65-68-71-73-74-77**
REARDON, Ray **1970-73-74-75-76-78**
REDGRAVE, Steven **1987-88-91**
REES, Leighton **1978**
REID, Brian **1985**
RENDLE, Sharon **1987-89**
RONALDSON, Chris **1981-85**
RONALDSON, Lesley **1987**
ROPER, David **1985**
ROUSE, Mick **1990**
ROWE, Arthur **1970**
ROWE, Diane **1954**
ROWE, Rosalind **1954**
RUSSELL, Mike **1989-90-91**
RUTTER, Tony **1984**

SANDERSON, Tessa **1984**
SANDFORD, Cecil **1952-57**
SANDO, Frank **1955-57**
SHAHER, Abdu **1988**
SHARMAN, Elizabeth **1983-87**
SHAW, Michael **1971**
SHAW, Norma **1981**
SHEEN, Gillian **1956**
SHEENE, Barry **1973-76-77**
SHEIL, Norman **1955-58**
SHEPHERD, Ann **1990**
SHOTTON, Sue **1984**
SIMES, Gary **1990**
SIMMONDS, Dave **1969**
SIMMONS, Malcolm **1976-77-78**
SIMPSON, Barry **1985**
SIMPSON, Tommy **1958-65**
SLY, Wendy **1983**
SMITH, A.J. **1987-89**

SMITH, Carl **1986**
SMITH, Cyril **1952**
SMITH, Jeff **1964-65**
SMITH, Joyce **1972**
SPALDING, Bob **1980-85**
SPENCER, John **1969-71-77**
SPINKS, Terry **1956**
SPRECKLEY, Brian **1985**
STEPHENS, Tim **1988**
STEVENS, Tony **1981-82-83-84-85-86**
STEWART, Ian **1975**
STEWART, Jackie **1969-71-73**
STEWART-WOOD, Jeanette **1967**
STRACEY, John H. **1975**
STURGESS, Colin **1989**
SULLIVAN, Terry **1985**
SURTEES, John **1956-58-59-60-64**
SUTHERLAND, Bob **1983**
SUTHERLAND, Murray **1984**

TAGG, Michael **1970**
TAYLOR, David **1968**
TAYLOR, Dennis **1985**
TAYLOR, Jock **1980**
TAYLOR, Phil **1990**
THOMAS, Dave **1981**
THOMAS, Paul **1956**
THOMPSON, Daley **1980-83-84**
THOMPSON, Don **1960**
THOMPSON, Jeoffrey **1982**
THORPE, David **1985**
TORVILL, Jayne **1981-82-83-84**
TOWLER, Diane **1966-67-68-69**
TRAIN, Andrew **1988**
TRAIN, Steve **1988**

WALTERS, John **1991**
WATSON, John **1982**
WATT, Jim **1979**
WEBB, Graham **1967**
WEBSTER, Jane **1980**
WEBSTER, Steve **1987-88-89-91**
WEIGHT, Pamela **1956**
WELLS, Allan **1980**
WEST, Jeremy **1976**
WEST, William **1976-80**
WESTWOOD, Jean **1952-53-54-55**
WHITBREAD, Fatima **1987**
WHITE, Jimmy **1980**
WHITE, Reg **1976**
WHITTALL, Robbie **1989-91**
WHITWELL, Alan **1986**
WIGG, Simon **1985-89-90**
WILDMAN, Mark **1984**
WILKIE, David **1973-75-76**
WILLIAMS, Freddie **1953**
WILLIAMS, Rex **1968-72-73-74-75-76-82-83**
WILLS, Phillip **1952**
WILSON, Cliff **1978**
WILSON, Jocky **1982-89**
WILSON, Michael **1982-83-88-89**
WILSON, Ray **1972**
WINSTONE, Howard **1968**
WOLSEY, Helen **1991**
WOOD, Robin **1987**
WOOSNAM, Ian **1987-90**

1952

NEWCASTLE won the Cup in 1952 for the second successive year, Churchill was back in Downing Street, The Times cost fourpence, the Daily Mirror a penny-halfpenny and at Helsinki a 1500-metre Olympic record was set: it was 13 seconds slower than Sebastian Coe was to run the distance 17 years later.

On the sixth of February, at the age of 25, Princess Elizabeth succeeded her father to the throne. The 40 years that followed were not always glorious for British sport, but not one of them was without glory. We have tried in these pages to record some of the greatest achievements, to recapture some of the unforgettable moments and to unearth some of the forgotten scenes from the sporting dramas of the time.

It is an ever-changing pageant. In this first year Wales won rugby's Grand Slam, British women golfers captured the Curtis Cup for the first time and Colin Cowdrey contested the final of the amateur rackets championship. Some things change very little: coming a close second in the Derby was a 16-year-old jockey named Lester Piggott.

Queen of Ice retires after Olympic triumph

JEANNETTE ALTWEGG remains Britain's greatest post-war solo female figure skater. The first of her four national titles was won in 1947 – the year she reached the final of the Wimbledon junior tennis championships. She won the world and European skating titles in 1951 and the Olympic gold in Oslo the following year. Despite tempting offers to turn professional, she immediately retired (at the age of 22) and went to teach in a Swiss orphanage.

Gold for Foxhunter

HARRY LLEWELLYN can hardly be separated in the public mind from Foxhunter, the horse bought by Colonel Llewellyn in 1947. Together they shared in the show jumping team bronze medal at the 1948 Olympics and the gold at Helsinki four years later. Llewellyn was a brilliant all-round rider, winning 140 international classes between 1947 and 1953 as well as 60 steeplechase events and second place in the 1936 Grand National.

Indians devastated by four-for-nought bowling blitz

FRED TRUEMAN was to become England's most famous fast bowler, but in the summer of this year the touring Indian side knew nothing of him (he had not been picked for the MCC tour to India the previous winter). In their second innings at Headingley four wickets fell before there was a run on the board. Trueman finished with 8 for 31 in 8.4 overs and took 29 wickets in the four-match series.

Cobb dies on Loch Ness

JOHN COBB, who had set a land speed record of 400 mph in 1947, attacked the water speed record on Loch Ness in 1952. It stood at 178.49mph. At his first attempt in September he reached 173.14 over the measured mile. Ten days later he tried again, entering the mile at a speed estimated at 240mph. Just before the end the boat pitched, bow down, and disintegrated. Cobb was killed and despite the average speed being logged at 206.89 mph, the record was not accepted.

CHAMPIONS OF THE WORLD

Cycling
Sprint - Reg Harris
Gliding
Open - Philip Wills
Ice Skating
Dance - Laurence Demmy and Jean Westwood
Motor Cycling
350cc - Geoff Duke
125cc - Cecil Sandford
Sidecar - Cyril Smith
Roller Skating
Dance - Ted Ellis and Marion Mercer
Snooker
Matchplay - Fred Davis

OLYMPIC CHAMPIONS

Ice Skating
Jeanette Altwegg
Show Jumping
Team - Great Britain

WORLD RECORDS

Athletics
Marathon (world best) - Jim Peters:
  2hr 20min 43sec.
4 x 200m relay, women - UK team:
  1min 39.7sec.
3 x 880yd relay, women - England team:
  7min 00.6sec.

1952 IS SPONSORED BY
COCA-COLA

"Coca-Cola" was first bottled in Great Britain in 1932, but with the advent of sugar rationing during World War 2, the world's favourite soft drink became unavailable.

In 1952, therefore, Coca-Cola was only just becoming re-established, but it was a momentous year in that franchise agreements were signed with the two major British companies that were to assist in the growth of the product over the next three decades.

Since 1987, this growth has increased dramatically. All production and distribution of "Coca-Cola" in this country has been carried out by Coca-Cola and Schweppes Beverages Limited, a joint venture company set up by The Coca-Cola Company and Cadbury Schweppes Plc.

The Coca-Cola Company has an established association with the major sporting activities throughout the world, resulting in a presence at such important events as the Olympic Games, the World Cup (FIFA), the Davis Cup and the Wimbledon Championships. Some years ago, a special office was set up in Europe to forge links with further events including the European Athletics Championships and the Tour de France.

In Great Britain we have had long relationships with many official sporting bodies, and currently sponsor the Football Association Coaching and Education Scheme, in addition to supporting the English, Scottish and Welsh national soccer teams. We are also closely involved with American Football at all levels throughout the country.

"Coca-Cola" is the world's favourite soft drink. It is a refreshing beverage – a small moment of pleasure to be enjoyed wherever and whenever people are having fun. It is only logical therefore, for The Coca-Cola Company and its products to be there, in more than 170 countries across the world.

1953

A SUITABLY glorious season of sport for Coronation year: a sensational Cup Final, an almost unbelievable Derby and the regaining of the cricketing Ashes that had been held by Australia since 1934. The monarch was Britain's youngest for more than a century, but this proved a year for ageing sports heroes.

Len Hutton, England's first professional captain, at 37 won back the Ashes and topped both Test and county batting averages. At 38, Stanley Matthews (with a little bit of help from his friends) won the Cup Final for Blackpool; at 49 Gordon Richards at last won the Derby in a thrilling battle with the Queen's horse, Aureole, just four days after Her Majesty was crowned; and on Coronation Day, aged 34, Edmund Hillary reached the peak of Everest.

It was an American who won the Open golf (Ben Hogan, aged 41) and two others who won the Wimbledon singles titles (Vic Seixas and Maureen Connolly). There was some cause there for the young to rejoice: 'Little Mo', that year the first woman ever to win the Grand Slam, was only 19. And at 23 Britain's Gordon 'Puff-Puff' Pirie was setting the first of his four world running records.

Derby win + Bookies caned as Gordon Richards beats Queen to Derby win + Bookies cane

HAD the Derby ever put the public in such a quandary? Four days after the Coronation, the Queen's celebrating subjects longed for her horse Aureole to win; with equal enthusiasm, their hearts and their shillings were behind Pinza and the great Gordon Richards, who at 49 was riding his last Derby – the only classic he had never won. Overnight the two contenders were 5-1 joint favourites. Sir Victor Sassoon's Pinza finished first, Aureole second.

The bookies lost millions, champagne was £2 12s 6d a bottle and the newly-knighted Sir Gordon Richards could retire content – but before he did, he became champion jockey for the 26th time in 29 years.

England win the Ashes

THE ASHES were contested in a dour series, with the first four Test matches drawn – thanks partly to rain and partly to batting of extraordinary patience that, at Lord's, brought Bailey 50 runs in 220 minutes and Willie Watson 109 in 345 minutes in a match-saving stand. Even Alec Bedser's 14 wickets for 99 at Trent Bridge was not enough to force a win.

At The Oval skipper Hutton saw it all come right. After 19 years, and on the fourth day of the final Test match of the summer, England regained the Ashes from Australia with an eight-wicket victory. This was Fred Trueman's first Australian Test, and Peter May's, but the executioners were the spinning 'twins', Laker and Lock. Between them, they took nine wickets for 120 runs in Australia's second innings.

Hutton's genius had flowered at The Oval 15 years earlier. This was where he made his world record Test score of 364, taking his average for that series against Australia past 118. By the time

he retired, he had scored a total of 6,971 runs in Test cricket, 2,428 of them against Australia.

Twice after the war he and Washbrook staged century opening partnerships in each innings of an Australian Test match. Against South Africa in Johannesburg they put on 359, then a Test record. England's first professional captain, Hutton led the side in 23 matches and never lost a series.

Matthews magic fills Cup

THE 1953 F.A. Cup Final is for ever remembered as the 'Matthews Final', though it was Stan Mortensen who scored a hat-trick for Blackpool (the only one in Cup Final history).

Bolton were 3-1 up with 22 minutes of the match remaining. Stanley Matthews curled one in from the right wing: Mortensen hit his second goal. Three minutes from time, he scored again, from a free kick: 3-3. Only seconds left and Matthews beat the full-back and speared a beautiful pass from the goal-line. Perry hit it and Matthews got his Cup-winners' medal at last.

World record falls

TWO of the greatest long-distance runners Britain ever produced were coming to their glorious best. Gordon Pirie, who ran for Britain in three Olympics and held the national cross-country title for three successive years, took his first world record in a six-mile race.

Four times as far suited Jim Peters better. Twice in 1953 he established world 'best times' for the marathon, but it was going to be the following year that he ran one of the most famous races in history.

CHAMPIONS OF THE WORLD

Athletics
Cross-country, team - England
Ice Skating
Dance - Lawrence Demmy and Jean Westwood
Pairs - John and Jennifer Nicks
Motor Cycling
500cc - Geoff Duke
350cc - Fergus Anderson
Sidecar - Eric Oliver
Snooker
Matchplay - Fred Davis
Speedway
Solo - Freddie Williams
Table Tennis
Team - England

WORLD RECORDS

Athletics
6 miles - Gordon Pirie: 28min 19.4sec.
Marathon (w.b.) - Jim Peters: 2hr 18min 41sec.
Marathon (w.b.) - Jim Peters: 2hr 18min 35sec.
4 x 1500m relay - UK team: 15min 27.2sec.
4 x 1 mile relay - UK team: 16min 41.0sec.
4 x 220yd relay, women - UK team: 1min 39.9sec.
3 x 880yd relay, women - England team: 6min 49.0sec.
Flying
Speed - Neville Duke: 727.6 mph.
Speed - Michael Lithgow: 735.7 mph.

1954

IF EVER failing memories were stirred by one athletics year, it would probably be this one. Here Roger Bannister destroyed the walls of his Jericho, the four-minute mile ('And the people shouted with a great shout, and the wall fell down flat'); here Jim Peters ran the most emotionally devastating marathon in history, and its most noble failure. And here, at London's White City Stadium, Chris Chataway ran the race of his life – perhaps the greatest 5,000-metre race ever to be run – to beat Vladimir Kuts to two world records.

This was the year too when England's identical table-tennis twins, Diane and Rosalind Rowe, won their world doubles (and on the other side of the net was Ann Haydon, 15 years away from winning Wimbledon). With another racket Geoffrey Atkins won his world championship, to retire undefeated 18 years later.

Not all went so well: England's footballers, beaten 7-1 by Hungary in Budapest, made it to the World Cup in Berne, but even with Finney, Matthews and Wright lost in the quarter-finals. Scotland had a more dramatic fall: they lost their first match, manager Andy Beattie resigned on the spot and the lads lost the next one 7-0 to Uruguay.

Bannister breaks four-minute barrier in world's greatest mile run

ROGER BANNISTER'S name is indelibly etched on the tablets of athletics. He had already brought his mile time down to 4min 2sec (the record was Gundar Haegg's at 4:1.4) when at Oxford University on 6 May 1954 Bannister, Chris Brasher and Chris Chataway executed their detailed plan to push Bannister under four minutes.
Brasher led them to a first lap of 57.5 and a second of 60.5. He gave way to Chataway, who took Bannister to the bell at 3:0.7 – seven-tenths of a second behind schedule. The last lap had to be run in 59 seconds. On the back straight Bannister's huge stride shot him to the front and on round the long, last bend into history: 3:59.4.

In the summer he ran 3:58.8 at the Commonwealth Games and in the last race of his life took the European Games 1500 metres title in 3:43.8.

Test record for Compton

DENIS COMPTON enjoyed his greatest cricketing days in the late 1940s, but in 1954 he made his highest Test score – 278 against Pakistan at Trent Bridge. Of those runs, 273 were made in one day, the most by any English Test batsman in England; and his 200 came up in 245 minutes – the fastest in English Test history since Wally Hammond's 240 minutes in 1933.

It was another 10 years before he was to retire from first-class cricket, by which time he had scored nearly 40,000 runs (5,807 of them in Tests).

Marathon tragedy for Peters at high noon in Vancouver

JIM PETERS was 35 when he captained the English athletics team to the Empire Games. In the previous two years he had four times set world best times for the marathon, bringing it down from 2hr 20min 43sec to 2:17:40. On the first Saturday in Vancouver he ran the six miles (bronze medal), on the second the marathon, starting in the blazing heat of noon. With three-quarters of a mile to go, Peters led the field by nearly three and a half miles – but he didn't know it. He came to the gates of the stadium at the limit of his endurance. 'Get this one over and we'll call it a day', he was saying to himself. He trotted uncertainly onto the track, with 380 yards to go and 35,000 people cheering him on. He fell over, got up, went on. He fell over again and again and again, reaching for the white tape that kept moving away from him. He passed out, never to run the marathon again. Eighteen minutes later a Scotsman, Joe McGhee, broke that tape.

Never Say Die Derby

LESTER PIGGOTT will feature again in these pages, but this was the year he won his first Derby, bringing home Never Say Die against the odds of 33-1. The horse, bred in America, gave Charlie Smirke his last St Leger win a few weeks later.

This was also the year Doug Smith succeeded Gordon Richards as champion flat jockey (after 12 consecutive years), Dick Francis became champion National Hunt rider and Her Majesty the Queen took the leading owner's berth with £40,993 in the bag.

CHAMPIONS OF THE WORLD

Athletics
Cross-country team - England

Cycling
Sprint - Reg Harris
Amateur sprint - Cyril Peacock

Ice Skating
Dance - Lawrence Demmy and Jean Westwood

Motor Cycling
500cc - Geoff Duke
350cc - Fergus Anderson

Rackets
Geoffrey Atkins

Rugby League
World Cup - Great Britain

Snooker
Matchplay - Fred Davis

Table Tennis
Doubles, women - Diane and Rosalind Rowe

WORLD RECORDS

Athletics
1 mile - Roger Bannister: 3min 59.4sec.
3 miles - Freddie Green: 13min 32.2sec.
3 miles - Chris Chataway: 13min 32.2sec.
3 miles - Chris Chataway: 13min 27.4sec.
5,000m - Chris Chataway: 13min 51.6sec.
Marathon (w. b.) - Jim Peters 2hr 17min 40sec.
880yd, women - Diane Leather: 2min 09.0sec.
3 x 880yd relay, women - UK team:
  6min 46.0sec.

Swimming
400yd ind. medley (short course) - Jack Wardrop:
  4min 41.7sec.

Q: What is the largest voluntary sports organisation in the world?

A: The Central Council of Physical Recreation

Made up of 198 British bodies and 64 English associations, the CCPR speaks for those twenty million sportsmen and sportswomen who regularly take part in organised sport and recreation in Britain. The CCPR is not a bureaucracy; it is the collective voice of the governing bodies who are responsible for the everyday running of their sport. From angling to speedway, from gardening to life saving, there is no recognised sport or recreational activity that does not come under the umbrella of the CCPR.

The CCPR represents
Because it is a democratic body, the CCPR knows immediately and exactly what the concerns of its members are. It can speak for them in the corridors of power; ministers and civil servants are left in no doubt as to the real issues which most concern sportsmen and sportswomen. Its voluntary character and freedom from central and local government direction, enables it to liaise with the media and present the true picture of sport.

The CCPR informs
Through its ever-expanding information services, it consistently keeps the sporting bodies and the general public up to date as to what is happening to, and within, sport.

The CCPR campaigns
Given the enormous contribution that sport makes to the social well-being of the nation, it is extraordinary that it should be under-financed. Indeed, through taxation, it is a net provider of revenue. This is just one of the anomalies that the CCPR aims to rectify in its many campaigns to protect the interests of sport.

The CCPR promotes
Its wide national and international contacts put the CCPR in an ideal position to mount a variety of projects, encouraging the wider participation of the nation in sport and active recreation.

1955

NAMES we have forgotten, and perhaps hardly knew, made marks on the sporting world of 1955 that are recalled now only by their nearest and dearest. The name of Diane Leather may ring a bell (two world running records), but in what field was Anne Shilcock's success? What did Roy Matthews do, and prove to be the last Briton to do it? How great, at what, was Jack Wardrop? And who remembers that James Dear this year succeeded as world real tennis champion the legendary Pierre Etchebaster, who retired undefeated at the age of 62, having held the title for 26 years?

Punters will more readily remember Pat Taafe's Grand National win on Quare Times, and as many followers of cricket that this was the end of Len Hutton's international career. He came back from the tour of New Zealand and Australia with five wins out of seven Tests, taking a wicket with the last ball of his last Test match.

He handed over to Peter May, who won the home series against South Africa (Trevor Bailey scored eight in 120 minutes at Headingley) as well as heading the first-class batting averages.

champion + More world records for Britain's great champion + More world record re

JACK WARDROP was an extraordinarily successful swimmer from Motherwell, in Scotland. He swam in the London Olympics of 1948 at the age of 16, and at Helsinki (1952) he and his brother Bert became (almost certainly) the only twins to win Olympic selection. That year Jack won all five British freestyle championships and set national records at every distance from 100 yards to a mile.

In 1954 he became the first British man for 40 years to break a world swimming record: the 400yd individual medley. In 1955 he set three more world records and in 1956 was picked for his third Olympic Games.

s + Five tries for Lions +

CLIFF MORGAN was the outstanding British fly-half of the decade, a rugby player of mesmerising brilliance who set the standard for the many fine fly-halves that Wales produced in the next 30 years. In the previous season he played a major part in the only defeats of the touring All-Blacks (by Cardiff and Wales), and in the summer of 1955 he was with the British Lions in South Africa.

The tourists won 18 of their 24 games and scored the record number of 94 tries. Five were in the first Test in Johannesburg, all of them made by Morgan and one scored by him. The 23-22 Lions victory was rated by those who saw it as one of the greatest internationals of all time.

+ Duke on top of the world again: fourth 500cc title in five years +

GEOFF DUKE was first of a magnificent run of British riders who dominated motor cycle racing for 20 years. This year was his last as a world champion (though he was only 32) and the fourth in five years in which he had won the sport's premier prize, the 500cc title. In 1952, the year he missed the 500, he took his second 350cc championship.

Between 1951, when Duke won his first 500cc world title, and 1965, when Mike Hailwood won his last, there were only three years when the crown did not go to a British rider. Italy's Agostini then took over, but there were still the years of Phil Read and Barry Sheene to come.

Since those glorious days, it has been only in sidecar motor cycling that Britain has triumphed.

+ All-British battle for Wimbledon doubles crown +

SURPRISINGLY, Angela Mortimer and Anne Shilcock remain the only all-British pair to have won the Wimbledon women's doubles title since the war and they did that by beating another British pair, Shirley Bloomer and Pat Ward, 7-5 6-1 in the final. Since that year, no British women's doubles partnership has reached the Wimbledon final, though some have made it with overseas partners.

Later to be crowned in the Wimbledon singles, Mortimer was much the steadier player (she won the French singles title in 1955 too) and Shilcock the ebullient and occasionally scintillating partner, one of the game's most attractive champions.

CHAMPIONS OF THE WORLD

Archery
Target - Roy Matthews
Target, team, women - Great Britain

Athletics
Cross-country - Frank Sando
Cross-country team - England

Cycling
Amateur pursuit - Norman Sheil

Ice Skating
Dance - Lawrence Demmy and Jean Westwood

Motor Cycling
500cc - Geoff Duke
350cc - Bill Lomas

Real Tennis
James Dear

Snooker
Matchplay - Fred Davis

Speedway
Peter Craven

WORLD RECORDS

Athletics
1500m, women - Diane Leather: 4min 25.0sec.
1 mile, women - Diane Leather: 4min 45.0sec.

Powerboating
Speed
Donald Campbell: 202.32 mph.
Donald Campbell: 216.20 mph.

Swimming
200m freestyle (short course) - Jack Wardrop: 2min 03.4sec
400yd individual medley (s.c.) - Jack Wardrop: 4min 36.9sec

1956

FIVE Olympic gold medals made a rich enough haul to put a smile on British faces (they included a world record swim by Judy Grinham in the 100 metres backstroke, a final with three British competitors and two medallists), but it was a cricket match that lifted the nation on to a cloud.

The Australians were here again, trying to get the Ashes back. They drew the first Test and won the second. Not so good. England recalled Washbrook, at 41. He made 98 at Headingley and England won by an innings, with Laker and Lock taking 18 wickets between them. And so to Old Trafford, where David Sheppard was recalled and scored 113 of England's 459.

In went the Australians and out for 84: Jim Laker took 9 for 37, including a spell of 22 balls when seven wickets fell for eight runs. In the second innings Laker bowled 51.2 overs for 53 runs and all 10 wickets, completing the greatest bowling performance of all time. Lock, the left-arm wizard, took 0-69 in 55 overs.

Rain shortened the final Test (for which Compton returned, at 38 and minus his right kneecap, to score 94) and it was drawn.

+ Brasher screams home for astonishing Olympic triumph +

CHRISTOPHER BRASHER'S steeplechase win at Melbourne was the least-expected triumph in the history of British athletics, and all the more inspiring for it. A marginal selection for the team, he won the final by nearly 15 yards in an Olympic record time of 8min 41.2 sec – six seconds faster than he had ever run before – and survived a protest to take the gold medal. It was the first Olympic athletics win for Britain since 1932.

Commenting on the Games, Harold Abrahams wrote: 'If a genius is one who has the capacity to take infinite pains, then Brasher is a genius.' The more obvious genius, Vladimir Kuts, stormed home in the 5,000 metres 11 seconds ahead of the next men, Gordon Pirie and Derek Ibbotson.

Historic British fencing

BORN on the same day as Brasher, fencer Gillian Sheen produced almost as great an Olympic surprise. British champion every year but one from 1949 to 1960, she was nevertheless given little chance of success in Melbourne. Though she won her first round pool, she was fourth in the next pool and had to fence-off to decide who went forward to the semi-final.

Her opponent was the reigning world champion, and Sheen won. In the final round, she lost her first bout and won the next six, to become the first (and still the only) British fencer of either sex to win Olympic gold.

Two boxing golds for Britain

SEVEN British boxers went to the Olympic Games and four of them came back with medals, an astounding achievement. Two were gold: in his first year of senior competition Terry Spinks *(above, left)* was the flyweight champion (he turned pro in 1957 and later became British featherweight champion); and Dick McTaggart, a sweet southpaw, took the lightweight title and the Val Barker trophy as the outstanding stylist of the Games.

Briton in two Wimbledon finals

ANGELA BUXTON, whose father owned the pier at Bognor Regis, was in two Wimbledon finals. She lost the singles to Shirley Fry and won the doubles with Althea Gibson, the first black player to be dominant in world tennis. The French singles title was won by Britain's Shirley Bloomer, soon to become Mrs Chris Brasher.

CHAMPIONS OF THE WORLD

Gliding
2-seater - Frank Foster and Nick Goodhart

Ice Skating
Dance - Paul Thomas and Pamela Weight

Motor Cycling
500cc - John Surtees
350cc - Bill Lomas

Snooker
Matchplay - Fred Davis

OLYMPIC CHAMPIONS

Athletics
Steeplechase - Chris Brasher

Boxing
Lightweight - Richard McTaggart
Flyweight - Terry Spinks

Fencing
Foil, women - Gillian Sheen

Swimming
100m backstroke, women - Judy Grinham

WORLD RECORDS

Athletics
3,000m - Gordon Pirie: 7min 55.6sec.
3,000m - Gordon Pirie: 7min 52.8sec.
5,000m - Gordon Pirie: 13min 36.8sec.
High jump, women - Thelma Hopkins: 1.74m.

Flying
Speed - Peter Twiss: 1,132 mph.

Swimming
100m backstroke, women - Judy Grinham: 1min 12.9sec.

1956 IS SPONSORED BY
REEBOK

NINETY-SEVEN GLORIOUS YEARS FOR REEBOK

1895
Joe Foster of the Bolton Primrose Harriers makes himself a pair of spike running 'pumps' and founds J.W. Foster & Sons – makers of sports shoes in Bolton, Lancashire.

1904
Alfred Shrubb – wearing a pair of Foster spikes breaks three world records during a 10 mile race on a rainy day at Ibrox Stadium.

1924
Eric Liddell, of Chariots of Fire fame, wins the 400m at the Paris Olympics wearing Foster's spikes.

1936
Jack Lovelock (NZ) wins the Olympic 1500m in a pair of Foster's spikes.

The De Lux Spike now costs 12/6d (63p) and Foster's make shoes for running, cycling, road-walking, boxing, soccer, and rugby at their Olympic Works in Bolton.

1952
John Disley, now director of Corporate Affairs for Reebok UK, wins the bronze medal in the 3000m steeplechase at the Helsinki Olympics.

1956
Christopher Brasher, now the chairman of Reebok UK, wins the Olympic gold medal in the 3000m steeplechase at Melbourne with a new Olympic record.

1958
'Young' Joe Foster – grandson of the founder – is now running the company and the name is changed to "Reebok". (Joe finds this name for a fast and agile gazelle in the dictionary).

1968
Dr Ron Hill breaks the World 10 miles Track Record in a pair of Reebok spikes.

1984
Steve Jones (Wales and RAF) sets the world's best time for the marathon – 2hr. 8min. 5sec – in Chicago wearing a pair of Reebok road-racing shoes made in Bolton.

1990
Reebok introduce the PUMP shoe with inflatable chambers designed to enhance fit and security.

The full circle from 'pumps' to PUMP is nearly a century of making sports shoes.

Reebok are still making quality sports shoes at their factory in Bolton, and are proud of their British heritage.

1957

GRAND SLAMS in rugby union – when one national side beats the other four in the Five Nations Championship – are rare enough to be remarkable. When England pulled it off at the beginning of this year it was their first since 1928 (though Wales had done it twice since the war) and they did it with some players who have become historic figures.

Eric Evans was coming to the end of a decade as hooker, with Ron Jacobs at prop, Marques and Currie at lock and Robbins at flank forward. Behind them was Jeeps, with Butterfield and W.P.C. Davies in the centre and Peter Jackson on the wing.

That was talent to compare with the England cricketers, who drew with South Africa away and beat the West Indies at home this year. The horse riders weren't bad either: Pat Smythe won the first of her three European show jumping championships on Flanagan, Scobie Breasley took the first of his flat jockey titles and the phenomenal Lester Piggott was hard at it: on Crepello to his second Derby and the 2,000 Guineas, and on the Queen's Carozza to take The Oaks – and to help Her Majesty to season's winnings of £62,211.

Scrum-half shows way ahead

DICK JEEPS suffered from some strange decisions by the England rugby selectors. He went to South Africa with the British Lions in 1955 and played in all four Tests – before he had played for England. When he came back they picked him for the first international and then dropped him, and it was not until 1957 that he was secure behind the England pack. He then became, and perhaps remains, the finest England scrum-half of the post-war era; and went on to become President of the Rugby Union and Chairman of the Sports Council.

England's massive total

TOM GRAVENEY'S batting record against the West Indies was tremendous and in this summer his average against them was 118. It was the year of Ramadhin and Valentine, but for the England side they held few terrors. England won the series 3-0, with two drawn.

Skipper May (285 not out) and Cowdrey (154) put on 411 for the fourth wicket at Edgbaston in a total of 583 for four wickets. At Trent Bridge England's massive 619 for six included a record second wicket partnership of 266 between Richardson (126) and Graveney (258) – his highest Test score.

...e way + For the third time Stirling Moss chases Fangio all the way + For the third t...

STIRLING MOSS was surely the greatest British racing driver never to win the world championship. From the age of 21 he was the nation's most successful track driver, and 1957 was the third successive year in which he finished second in the Grand Prix championship to Fangio. He was second the following year too (to Mike Hawthorn) and then third for three years – never out of the top three for seven consecutive years.

Moss's record, and the appeal of his personality, ensured that he remained a British sporting star many years after he stopped competing. Favourite circuit: Goodwood, where he won races from 1947 to its closure in 1966.

Campbell and Bluebird fly to another world record + Ca...

DONALD CAMPBELL inherited the extraordinary determination of his father, Britain's most famous pre-war racing motorist, to travel faster than any other man on earth – or more particularly, on the water. Malcolm set the land speed record of 245.70 mph in 1931, was afterwards knighted and then turned his attention to speedboats.

After his father's death, Donald pursued similar goals and gave the same name, Bluebird, to the jet-powered boats he built. In this year he twice raised his water speed record, to 239 mph, and continued to do so until his death on Coniston Water 10 years later.

CHAMPIONS OF THE WORLD

Athletics
Cross-country - Frank Sando

Ice Skating
Dance - Courtney Jones and June Markham

Motor Cycling
250cc - Cecil Sandford

Real Tennis
Albert Johnson

Snooker
Matchplay - John Pulman

WORLD RECORDS

Athletics
1 mile - Derek Ibbotson: 3min 57.2sec

Powerboating
Speed - Donald Campbell: 225.63 mph.
Speed - Donald Campbell: 239.07 mph.

1958

CARDIFF'S Commonwealth Games, European athletics championships in Stockholm, the football World Cup in Switzerland and a Test series against New Zealand gave sports fans plenty to read about this year. With the exception of Arthur Rowe, Britain's track and field athletes fared much better in Europe than they did at Cardiff, where Herb Elliott and Milkha Singh were rampant; but in the pool, Judy Grinham and Anita Lonsbrough were unbeatable, both setting world records. Equally triumphant was a lad named Brian Phelps, who at the age of 14 won the European high diving championship.

New Zealand were five times dismissed for less than 100 runs, Tony Lock finished the series with 34 wickets at an average of 7.47, and Arthur Milton made his Test debut with a not out century. Matters went pretty well on the tennis court too: Britain had a Wimbledon singles finalist and won the Wightman Cup for the first time since 1930.

This was the year of the Manchester United air crash, but there was something to celebrate in football. For the first time the British nations were put in separate qualifying groups for the World Cup and all four made it to the finals.

ry + Wales close to glory

JOHN CHARLES of Juventus, a magnificent footballer, was the figurehead of Wales's progress to the quarter-finals of the World Cup. Having beaten Hungary in extra time, they went down 1-0 to Brazil, eventual winners of the tournament.

Ireland reached the quarters too, losing 4-0 to France, but neither Scotland nor England (with a squad that included Bobby Charlton, Johnny Haynes, Don Howe and Bobby Robson) won a match in their groups.

Teenager's triple triumph + Teenager's

JUDY GRINHAM this year became the only swimmer in history to hold Olympic, European and Commonwealth Games titles at the same time. She had won an Olympic title in 1956 (the first British swimmer to do so for 32 years) with a world record time for 100m backstroke of 1min 12.9sec. She cut that to 1:11.9 at the European championships in Budapest in 1958 and won the 110yd backstroke at the Cardiff Commonwealth Games. The next year, on her twentieth birthday, she retired. The last British backstroke swimmer to be a world beater, Judy Grinham is one of the few sports stars to have married a sports writer.

...an Cup + Truman the star as Britain take Wightman Cup

SEVENTEEN-year-old Christine Truman established herself as the darling of British tennis when she won all her matches in the Wightman Cup at Wimbledon. They included one against Althea Gibson, who a month later was to beat Angela Mortimer (not picked for the Wightman team) in the Wimbledon final. Britain won by four matches to three, with Ann Haydon (later Ann Jones) winning the deciding singles against Mimi Arnold.

European gold for Rowe +

ARTHUR ROWE was Britain's only male athlete to win gold medals at both the Commonwealth Games and the European championships of 1958, at the surprisingly early age for a shot putter of 22. He also set a new European record of 64ft 2in.

He later played briefly in professional rugby league before most successfully joining the Scottish professional games circuit and dominating their heavy field events.

CHAMPIONS OF THE WORLD

Athletics
Cross-country - Stan Eldon
Cross-country team - England

Cycling
Pursuit - Tommy Simpson
Amateur pursuit - Norman Sheil

Fencing
Epee - Bill Hoskyns

Golf
World Cup - Ireland

Ice Skating
Dance - Courtney Jones and June Markham

Motor Cycling
500cc - John Surtees
350cc - John Surtees

Motor Racing
Grand Prix - Mike Hawthorn

Roller Skating
Dance - Sydney and Patricia Cooper

Table Tennis
Team, women - England

WORLD RECORDS

Athletics
440yd, women - Molly Hiscox: 55.6sec.
4 x 110yd relay, women - England: 45.3sec.

Swimming
100m backstroke, women - Margaret Edwards: 1min 12.4sec.
100m backstroke, women - Judy Grinham: 1min 11.9sec.
220yd breaststroke, women - Anita Lonsbrough: 2min 53.5sec.
4 x 100m relay, women - United Kingdom team: 4min 54.0sec.

1958 IS SPONSORED BY
DAN-AIR

DAN-AIR, the Gatwick-based airline, is the UK's second biggest scheduled international carrier. It has more scheduled routes to Continental Europe than any other Gatwick airline.

Summer 1992 is particularly busy for Dan-Air as its route network has been expanded to include six new services serving Athens, Barcelona, Rome and Stockholm, and, later this year, Cairo and Istanbul.

At the same time many frequencies have been stepped up and now provide improved connections at Gatwick for both incoming and departing passengers and on both Dan-Air and its interline partners.

Six new Boeing 737s have joined the Dan-Air fleet this year and an additional six BAe 146-300 aircraft have been ordered. By 1995 the average age of the fleet will be down to 5.4 years.

Almost all Dan-Air's international scheduled services offer a choice of Class Elite – a highly regarded business class – and Economy with a full range of fares offered.

Dan-Air, which was founded in 1953, is owned by Davies & Newman Holdings plc, which is quoted on the London Stock Exchange.

Dan-Air celebrates its own 40 Glorious years.

Key Dates
1953 Founded by London shipbroker.
1956 First scheduled service (to Jersey).
1960 Moved to Gatwick – the new airport opened by the Queen.
1966 The first of 49 Comet aircraft introduced.
1971 Became first UK airline to be publicly quoted on Stock Exchange.
1973 First airline to introduce Boeing 727s.
1983 Launch operator of BAe 146 – later adopted by the Queen's Flight.
1988 Business Class introduced on scheduled services.
1991 Became UK's second largest international scheduled carrier and largest operator from Gatwick Airport.
1992 Seven new scheduled routes added; six new aircraft introduced.
1993 40th Anniversary.

1959

AS THIS decade comes to a close, Fred Trueman deserves a special word. Seven years earlier, he had been let loose on Test cricket for the first time and had petrified the touring Indians. In 1959 they returned and found him still at it, and though the improved pitches enabled them to cope with him rather better, he still took 24 wickets in England's record 5-0 series win.

Trueman was to go on playing Test cricket another six years, harvesting a total of 307 wickets – far more than any other fast bowler in the world, and at a lower average than his great contemporaries. As John Arlott said, when the fire burned he was as fine a fast bowler as ever lived.

Allan Jay had fire too: he won the world foil fencing championship this year and was second (by only one hit) in the epee competition. The queen of British cycling, Beryl Burton, also took her first world championship in 1959, and over on the grassy slopes of Lisbon England's cross-country runners were at their very best, with four men in the first five of the world championship. Success was nothing new to them: in the 20 years between 1953 and 1972 they won the team prize 16 times.

of the world + Mighty Martin lifts Britain to the top of the world + Mighty Martin l

LOUIS MARTIN, the greatest weightlifter Britain has produced, won the first of his four world championships this year. He went on to win gold medals in three successive Commonwealth Games, bronze and silver medals in the Olympics of 1960 and 1964, and to set more than 100 world, Olympic, European, Commonwealth and British records.

Martin, who was born in Jamaica, weighed about 14 stone. Yet in the Tokyo Olympics the combined weight of his two lifts was 1,047 lb – an average of nearly twice his own weight at each lift.

No other British weightlifter has since won a world or Olympic title, though the diminutive Precious McKenzie became almost as well-known as Louis Martin for his four successive Commonwealth Games gold medals between 1966 and 1978 – the last of them after he had emigrated to New Zealand.

Courtney Jones dances to gold with different partner

FOR most of us, ice dancing did not exist until Torvill and Dean – and then only thanks to television. But Britain ruled the world at this sport for many years. Lawrence Demmy and Jean Westwood were world champions for four consecutive years from 1952 (as were Torvill and Dean 30 years later); from 1957 Courtney Jones held the title for four years with two different partners, June Markham and Doreen Denny *(right)*; and Bernard Ford and Diane Towler had four years of triumph from 1966, when a journalist reporting their win noted that they were 'displaying well-unified body sways.'

Some reporters have become rather more sophisticated in their pronouncements, but the armchair fan needs to know few subtleties to revel in great ice dancing.

There are three sections in an international competition: the compulsories, in which three precisely prescribed dances have to be executed, worth 30 per cent of the overall points; the original set pattern dance (20 per cent), in which the tempo is prescribed but not the composition of the dance; and the best-known element, the four minutes of free skating (50 per cent of the overall points).

Two marks, for technical merit and for artistic impression, are given by nine judges. The maximum is 6.0, for a 'perfect and flawless' performance.

Extraordinary double for the barnacle of England

TREVOR BAILEY was often mocked during his 10 years of Test cricket. 'Barnacle' Bailey he was called, for the dour tenacity of his batting. On the tour to Australia in the 1958-59 winter, for instance, an innings of 68 lasted more than seven and a half hours of the first Test in Brisbane – where England totalled only 106 in a day's batting. They lost the Ashes.

But in this summer of 1959 Bailey became the first cricketer since 1937 to score 2,000 runs and take 100 wickets in a season. He achieved the 1,000/100 double eight times and in his first-class career scored 28,642 runs and took 2,082 wickets. In his greatest day of bowling, he took seven West Indies wickets for 34 runs in 16 overs.

CHAMPIONS OF THE WORLD

Athletics
Cross-country - Fred Norris
Cross-country team - England

Canoeing
Slalom K1 - Paul Farrant

Cycling
Pursuit, women - Beryl Burton

Fencing
Foil - Allan Jay

Ice Skating
Dance - Courtney Jones and Doreen Denny

Motor Cycling
500cc - John Surtees
350cc - John Surtees

Weightlifting
90k - Louis Martin

WORLD RECORDS

Swimming
400m individual medley - Ian Black: 5min 08.8sec.
200m breaststroke, women - Anita Lonsbrough: 2min 50.3sec.

1960

NO WAY of hiding disappointment over British results in the Rome Olympics, which produced only two gold medals (walker Don Thompson and swimmer Anita Lonsbrough); but a search for threads of triumph reveals that of the five silvers, Allan Jay's was the first medal ever won by a male fencer and that of the 12 bronze, Brian Phelps secured the first British male diving medal in Olympic history.

Gordon Pirie did not make the 5,000 metre final, nor Arthur Rowe the last round of the shot; and Britain's sprinting star Peter Radford, who earlier in the year set a world 200m record, came home with a bronze in the 100m. Eight of the British medals were won by women, with Dorothy Hyman taking silver and bronze in the two sprints.

On the cricket ground England won series against the West Indies away and South Africa at home; on the football field Wolves, who had taken the League in 1959, won the Cup in 1960 – and have never won either since; and on the race track Piggott took his third Derby (the fifth for owner Sir Victor Sassoon) and his first flat championship.

medal + 'The Little Mouse' climbs the highest mountain to win Olympic gold medal + '

DON THOMPSON was christened 'Il Toppolino' by the Italian press at the Rome Olympics – 'the little mouse'. The smallest and slightest member of the British athletics team, he conquered the highest mountain: the 50 kilometre walk, more than 31 miles. For him, no great distance: he had nine times won the London to Brighton walk and twice the Milan 100km.

Four years earlier, the Olympic dream of the London insurance clerk had turned to a nightmare in the heat of Melbourne. To cope with the heat of Rome he converted his bathroom at home into a tropical hothouse and trained by running on the spot in humid temperatures of up to 100 degrees Fahrenheit; and on the day he wore large sunglasses and a Foreign Legion type of headdress. It worked.

Diving history for Phelps

THOUGH the Olympic medal won by Brian Phelps was of bronze, it held more than usual significance: he became the first British man to win any medal in diving. In British terms, Phelps had a sensational record: he was only 14 when he won his first European highboard diving championship and he was twice a double gold medallist in Commonwealth Games.

Like many divers, Phelps often trained on a trampoline. After retiring from competition, he formed and ran a trampoline club in Poole, Dorset, which became a nursery for many of the best young performers in the land.

+ World record win for British swimmer in Rome + Worl

ANITA LONSBROUGH was the last British woman to win an Olympic swimming gold medal, and that was in 1960. After being two seconds down at the halfway stage of the 200 metres breaststroke, the Huddersfield teenager won by half a second, setting a world record of 2min 49.5sec – an entire length of the pool faster than the time in which the race had last been won by a Briton.

Lonsbrough did not turn seriously to the breaststroke until she was 16, but within nine months she had won her first Commonwealth Games title. In 1962 she retained that, won the European 200m and added both the Commonwealth 110-yard breaststroke and the 440-yard individual medley.

+ Burton rides to the top

IN THE nine years from 1959 to 1967, cyclist Beryl Burton won nine world championships on track and road, outstandingly the best record in the history of the sport. In this year of 1960 she won two of them and set a world record for 20 kilometres. In domestic sport, she consistently out-rode the best men in long distance events. She was British all-round time-trial champion for 24 successive years, taking her up to the age of 45.

CHAMPIONS OF THE WORLD

Billiards
Amateur - Herbert Beetham

Cycling
Pursuit, women - Beryl Burton
Road race, women - Beryl Burton

Ice Skating
Dance - Courtney Jones and Doreen Denny

Motor Cycling
500cc - John Surtees
350cc - John Surtees

Rugby League
World Cup - Great Britain

OLYMPIC CHAMPIONS

Athletics
50km walk - Don Thompson

Swimming
200m breaststroke, women - Anita Lonsbrough

WORLD RECORDS

Athletics
200m - Peter Radford: 20.5sec.
220yd - Peter Radford: 20.5sec.
880yd, women - Joy Jordan: 2min 06.1sec.

Cycling
20km, women - Beryl Burton: 28min 58.4sec.

Swimming
200m breaststroke, women - Anita Lonsbrough: 2min 49.5sec.

1960 IS SPONSORED BY
SCOTTISH & NEWCASTLE plc

IN 1960 Scottish Brewers, with its headquarters in Edinburgh, joined forces with Newcastle Breweries in the North East of England, to form Scottish & Newcastle Breweries.

The two companies had been trading across the border into each other's locations for many years and the logical merger brought together two great brewing companies – Scottish Brewers famous for its McEwans and Youngers beers and Newcastle Breweries for its world renowned Newcastle Brown Ale.

During the past 32 years, the company has developed into a Brewing, Retail and Leisure group now known simply as Scottish & Newcastle plc. It operates five breweries in Britain, runs 2,000 pubs and supplies some 20,000 'free trade' and supermarket customers. On the leisure front, S&N owns Holiday Club Pontin's and the European short break holiday specialists, Centre Parcs.

Throughout its history, Scottish & Newcastle has always maintained strong links with the various communities in which it works and trades, through sporting events and activities.

Its 'Support for Sport' programme is administered via its Trading Companies which operate throughout the UK – Scottish Brewers in Scotland, Newcastle Breweries in North East England, Wm Younger and Theakstons in Yorkshire, Matthew Brown in the North West, Home Brewery in the Midlands and Youngers in the South.

Scottish & Newcastle's 'helping hand' touches a wide range of sports from soccer to sailing, cricket to curling, horse racing to hockey and athletics to angling. The list seems endless.

Support is directed at grass-roots level as part of the company's community involvement plan, as well as major sponsorship of football teams such as Glasgow Rangers, Newcastle United, Blackburn Rovers and Notts County.

Scottish & Newcastle recently sponsored the Scottish team to the Commonwealth Games, but is equally at home helping with the local scene, creating the champions of tomorrow.

1961

BRITAIN had produced only four world boxing champions since the end of the war, and the last had been middleweight Randolph Turpin 10 years earlier, so there was some cause for celebration when Terry Downes took that title from Paul Pender in 1961; and rather more when two Britons contested the Wimbledon women's singles final.

Elsewhere sporting joy was on the sparse side. The Australian cricketers came and retained the Ashes, in Peter May's last series as captain. Trueman did his best to stop them at Headingley. He took five for 38 in the first innings, all five falling in six overs with the second new ball for only 16 runs. In the second innings he devastated them with off-cutters: he took five wickets without conceding a run, finishing with six for 30.

The Derby was won by Psidium, a 66-1 outsider from France, but two home-grown riding talents did show themselves this year, both at the age of 21. David Broome followed his Olympic bronze medal on Sunsalve by winning the European show jumping championship, and Mike Hailwood took his 250cc Honda to the first of his nine world crowns.

+ All-British Wimbledon final + All-Brit

HISTORY was made at Wimbledon, with the only post-war final between British players. It was Angela Mortimer's second singles final (she had also won the French title in 1955 and the Australian in 1958), and Christine Truman's only one. The British public were ecstatic and, as usual, wanted the younger girl to win. Her chances were not helped by a fall on court and Mortimer scraped home 4-6, 6-4, 7-5, to receive the trophy from Princess Alice, Countess of Athlone.

With the two Wimbledon finalists and Ann Haydon (the French champion) in the Wightman Cup team, the inexperienced Americans were not given a chance of regaining the trophy. But it was a Chicago massacre: 6-1 to the US.

+ Test sun sets on May +

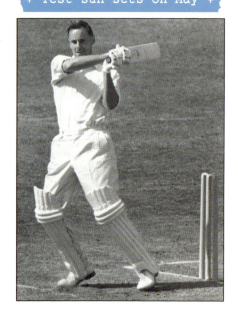

PETER MAY'S place in cricket history was secure, though this summer he played the last of his 66 Test matches at the early age of 32 . His captaincy record was remarkable: 41 matches and 10 series, of which he won seven.

Some rate him the finest of all post-war batsmen. He scored more than 4,500 Test runs, with 13 centuries and an average of nearly 47, and his straight driving was as beautiful a sight as cricket could offer. His England debut firmly established his Test career: 138 against South Africa at Headingley in 1951, when he was 22.

The most memorable of all his innings was a prodigious 285 not out against the West Indies in 1957 (the highest score of his career). England were 288 behind on the first innings, when May and Cowdrey put on 411 for the fourth wicket. May's average for that series (won 3-0 by England) was 97.80 runs.

Spurs' great soccer double

DANNY BLANCHFLOWER led Tottenham Hotspur to the first double this century of Football League championship and F.A. Cup. Domestic though the triumph is, it signifies greatness and international stature. Spurs won the League with a record number of wins — 31 out of their 42 matches, taking their points to equal the Arsenal record of 64 in 1931.

Blanchflower's inspiring captaincy (he also led Ireland) more than compensated for the fact that he might no longer be the best wing-half in the business. Spurs were more than enough for Leicester City at Wembley, winning 2-0, but lost to Benfica in the semi-final of the European Cup a year later.

Downes regains world title in return with Pender

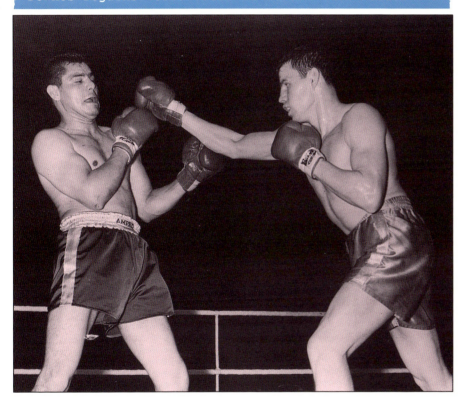

TERRY DOWNES later made something of a face for himself in British films, but in the early 1960s he had his hands full with a series of world title fights against Paul Pender (who had twice beaten Sugar Ray Robinson).

Downes *(on the right, above)* lost to Pender in the States, but on the return in London in July 1961 forced the American to retire in the ninth round. Pender regained the crown with a points win in Boston the next year, after which Downes moved up to light-heavyweight and unsuccessfully challenged Willie Pastrano for that title.

CHAMPIONS OF THE WORLD

Athletics
Cross-country - Basil Heatley
Race walking, team - United Kingdom
Boxing
Middleweight - Terry Downes
Canoeing
Canoe sailing - Alan Emus
Motor Cycling
250cc - Mike Hailwood

WORLD RECORDS

Athletics
10 miles - Basil Heatley: 47min 47.0sec.
Gliding
Height gain, women - Anne Burns: 29,918ft.

1961 IS SPONSORED BY
BUTLINS

BUTLIN'S has become very much a part of British heritage since it first opened its doors to the British holidaymaker, 56 years ago.

Then, Sir Billy Butlin's dream was to offer an affordable, fun-packed holiday, and that principle is still in the forefront of development today. As the holiday market has changed, Butlin's has remained dedicated to its customers' enjoyment and has always played a significant role in the community, a tradition which still exists today.

Part of Butlin's progress is a commitment to the development of sport for children in Britain and they are proud to be associated with the CCPR National Pentathlete Award Scheme which helps to extend sports involvement at a grass roots level throughout the country. The sponsorship programme also includes practical involvement in providing valuable specialist sports training to children of all ages.

Butlin's are pleased that this sponsorship will help to achieve the objectives of the CCPR, to build and develop interest and achievement in all sporting areas, and will help young people to develop fitness and become involved in sport.

1962

BRITAIN'S athletes were busy and successful at the European Games this year (five track gold medals) and at the Commonwealth Games in Australia, where two of our swimmers won five gold medals between them and in a quiet corner the bowls was won by David Bryant – still a world champion 30 years later.

Fred Winter, one of the greatest of all steeplechase jockeys, had a tremendous season. He won his second Grand National (on Kilmore), the Cheltenham Gold Cup and the Grand Steeplechase de Paris on a mount with a broken bit. In a disastrous Derby, Neville Selwood was one of the few happy jockeys, winning on Larkspur.

Rod Laver completed one of the rare Grand Slams of tennis, and in golf there was more from the Americans: Arnold Palmer won The Open again and the US Open went to Jack Nicklaus, who the previous year (then only 21) had been playing for the amateurs in the Walker Cup.

Ipswich Town are worth a mention: under manager Alf Ramsey they came up from the Third Division to win the Second in 1961 and the League Championship in 1962. By the end of the year Ramsey had been appointed England manager.

Hill and his BRM climb to the top of the Grand Prix pile

GRAHAM HILL'S Grand Prix drivers' championship win this year heralded an extraordinary run of British success in the sport. In 12 years the nation was to provide eight world champions and seven runners-up. With three wins in Europe and one in South Africa in 1962, Hill kept his nose ahead of Scotland's Jim Clark.

Hill came into the sport as a mechanic and did not race until he was 27. From 1960 to 1966 he drove for BRM, and followed his first place with three successive seconds, all of them behind other British drivers. In a Lotus, he beat Jackie Stewart to the championship in 1968.

Hill took the Monaco Grand Prix five times, but never once the British. Though he later broke both legs in a crash, he returned to the track to continue driving. He ranks as the second most successful British racing driver of all time.

Hyman's gold hat trick

DOROTHY HYMAN was a rare specimen: a truly world-class British female sprinter. In 1962 she took gold medals in both Commonwealth Games sprints, and in the 100 metres (11.3sec) at the European championships in Belgrade. She won three Olympic medals, a British sprinting record: in 1960 (Rome) the 100m silver and the 200m bronze, and in 1964 (Tokyo) a bronze in the 4 x 100m relay team.

Greaves strikes in World Cup battle with Brazil

THIS was World Cup football time again, in Chile, but the only British side to get there was England, who in the first pool of the final tournament lost to Hungary, drew with Bulgaria and beat Argentina 3-1. Haynes and Bobby Charlton were prominent, but the prime goal-scorer of his day was inside-forward Jimmy Greaves *(above)*. Though he could not get England past Brazil in the quarter-finals (1-3), his strike rate is not easily forgotten.

He was only 20 when, in 1960, he scored his 100th League goal for Chelsea (his first club). Three years later he scored his 200th, for Spurs, and made it 220 before he left them. He was five times the League's top scorer, setting a post-war First Division record of 41 in the 1960-61 season.

Ludgrove does the double

LINDA LUDGROVE had succeeded Judy Grinham as Britain's outstanding backstroke swimmer, and she won both gold medals (110 and 220 yards) in the Commonwealth Games of 1962 and 1966. An even more exciting achievement in the pool came from Anita Lonsbrough, who not only won her two breaststroke events at Perth, but also the 440yd individual medley.

CHAMPIONS OF THE WORLD

Athletics
Cross-country, team - England
Cycling
Pursuit, women - Beryl Burton
Motor Cycling
500cc - Mike Hailwood
Motor Racing
Grand Prix - Graham Hill
Roller Skating
Dance - Brian and Patricia Colclough
Speedway
Peter Craven
Weightlifting
90kg - Louis Martin

WORLD RECORDS

Athletics
80m hurdles, women - Barbara Moore: 10.5sec (equal)

Chaos at the Derby this year: seven horses fell at Tattenham Corner, including the favourite, Hethersett. Ryan Price's King Canute II was destroyed on the course, six jockeys were taken to hospital and four detained.

ADT HEALTHQUEST

ADT HEALTHQUEST is a charitable trust which promotes the benefits of active, healthy living and raises funds for other health-related charities. Three major national organisations work in close partnership with Healthquest – the Central Council of Physical Recreation, the Fitness Industry Association and the Health Education Authority.

Healthquest aims to heighten public awareness about the importance of moderate, regular exercise combined with sensible, balanced diets. Sebastian Coe, former Olympic athlete, identified the need for a national campaign to try to reduce the incredibly high premature death rates in the UK from coronary heart disease, many of which have preventable causes – overweight, too little exercise, high blood cholesterol levels etc. Whilst the UK was, and remains, a nation of sports lovers with some incredible achievements over the years, too many people, of all ages and backgrounds, neglect their own health and fitness.

The Healthquest Charitable Trust, chaired by Sebastian Coe, was officially launched in February 1991 with generous sponsorship from ADT, the world leader in electronic security services and vehicle auctions. Above all, the Healthquest campaign seeks to show that living a healthy and active life can be fun, requires only relatively small changes in living patterns, and is within everyone's grasp.

In its first year Healthquest ran a national roadshow touring the country, with support from Tesco, and the "Commit To Get Fit" event was held at FIA member clubs. Healthquest will build on those initiatives in future years – putting the life back into living.

For more information write to:
ADT Healthquest,
PO Box 293A, Surbiton,
Surrey KT5 8DA.

1963

TEN years after the Coronation, some sports still hung on to the 'gentlemen and players' concept. Though it was a good many years since professional cricketers were forced to leave the field of play at Lord's by a side gate, the influential men of the game remained (after Len Hutton's retirement) the gentlemen of Oxbridge, who continued to provide the captaincy for which they had been groomed.

Tennis, through its International Federation rather than the British establishment, resolutely refused to go 'open' and preferred to pay so-called amateurs large expenses rather than admit professionals to tournaments such as Wimbledon. The greatest players of the day tended to move out of the 'amateur' ranks when they had reached their peak, responding to invitations to join the highly-paid professional circus. So it was that Rod Laver, who in 1962 had won the Grand Slam, did not defend his Wimbledon title and was succeeded by a player of lesser rank, Chuck McKinley.

Soccer had not been like that since 1885. Tottenham Hotspur were still revelling in glory, and this year became the first British side to win the European Cup-Winners' Cup (5-1 against Atletico Madrid).

ians + England spirits raised as Dexter lords it over the West Indies + England spir

ONE of the most heroic figures of post-war English cricket, 'Lord' Ted Dexter captained England in seven Test series between 1961 and 1964. His apparently cavalier attitude and the power of his driving raised the excitement level at any ground on which he strode out to bat.

His highest Test score was 205 against Pakistan in Karachi and his most memorable innings a disciplined, match-saving 174 in eight hours against Australia at Old Trafford in 1964; but those who saw his fearless 70 at Lord's in this year of 1963, against the fiery might of the West Indians, will need some persuading that he ever played more brilliantly.

Dexter surprisingly made his first representative mark as a bowler. Playing for the Gentlemen (of course) against the Players at Lord's in 1957, he returned the extraordinary analysis of five wickets for eight runs in the first innings and 3 for 47 in the second. As a medium-pace change bowler, he later took 66 wickets for England and more than 300 for Sussex, which he captained from 1960 to 1965.

He stood as a Conservative parliamentary candidate in Cardiff (losing to James Callaghan), was run over by his own car, raced horses and dogs and pulled out of cricket in his prime. Ted Dexter was an outstanding amateur golfer and probably still is, though in recent years he has been better known as the overlord of English Test cricket.

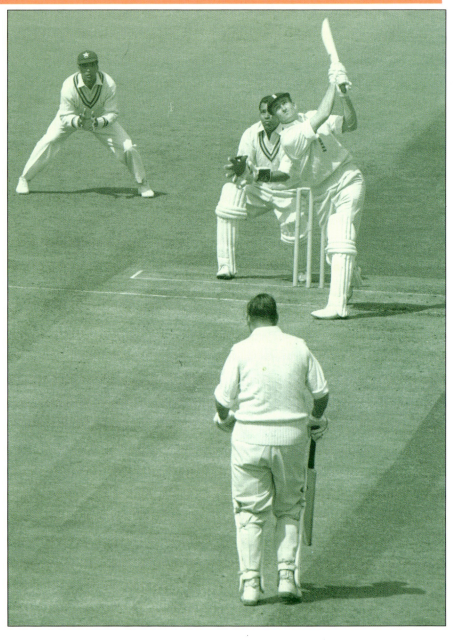

Atkins reigns supreme

THERE have been only 23 holders of the world rackets title since 1820 and nobody held it as long as did Geoffrey Atkins. He was the British, American and Canadian amateur singles champion when, in 1952, he challenged James Dear for the world championship and won it by the narrowest of margins. Atkins *(below left with Dear)* surrendered it, undefeated, in 1971 at the age of 44.

In those 20 years Atkins was challenged only four times and never beaten. The first of the challenges, by James Leonard, came in 1963 and was swept aside 6-1. This same year, as if to reinforce his domination, Atkins also won the United Kingdom amateur singles at rackets (for the fifth time) and at real tennis (for the third).

Pat Smythe takes Flanagan to the top again

EQUALITY of the sexes in equestrian events is now so taken for granted that it is hard to remember that for a long time men and women were treated as different animals in show jumping (though not in eventing). It was 1956 before women were admitted to the Olympic Games in that sport, and Pat Smythe was immediately picked for the British team. On Flanagan, she helped the nation to a team bronze medal.

She became the most successful female show jumper of her time, winning the women's European championship in 1957 and again for three consecutive years, from 1961 to 1963 – every time with Flanagan. Smythe won the British women's championship a record eight times between 1952 and 1962.

Scot swims fastest 100 metres in the world

BOBBY McGREGOR is the only British swimmer to have won an Olympic freestyle sprint medal in the history of the Games, and was the first man to win any swimming medal since 1912. In 1963 the Scot broke the world record for the 100m (54sec), but next year in Tokyo the euphoria over Britain's athletic successes was so great his achievement there was overshadowed. He was beaten for the gold medal by only a touch and the winner, Don Schollander (US), set a new world record of 53.4sec.

CHAMPIONS OF THE WORLD

Angling
Freshwater - William Lane

Athletics
Cross-country - Roy Fowler
Race walking, team - United Kingdom

Cycling
Pursuit, women - Beryl Burton

Motor Cycling
500cc - Mike Hailwood

Motor Racing
Grand Prix - Jim Clark

Rackets
Geoffrey Atkins

Roller Skating
1000m, road - Danny Kelly

Snooker
Amateur - Gary Owen

Weightlifting
90kg - Louis Martin

WORLD RECORDS

Athletics
4 x 110yd relay - United Kingdom: 40.0sec (equal)
4 x 110yd relay, women - United Kingdom: 45.2sec.

Swimming
100m freestyle - Bobby McGregor: 54.0sec.

1964

FOR Britain, the most exciting Olympics since the war were held in Tokyo, where in the athletics stadium the UK won a totally unexpected four gold medals and seven silver. As well as the famous Lynn Davies, Ann Packer and Mary Rand victories, don't forget Ken Matthews, one-and-a-half minutes clear of the field in the 20 kilometre walk. Paul Nihill was only 20 seconds off gold in the 50km walk and the men's 4 x 400 metre relay team exceeded the previous world record though they were second to the United States.

Earlier in the year at Innsbruck, Tony Nash and Robin Dixon won the two-man bob gold medal, to become (and to remain) the only British champions off the ice rink in the history of the Winter Olympics.

Notable deeds at home included Ken Barrington's 256 against the Australians at Old Trafford, Scobie Breasley winning his first Derby at the age of 50 (on Santa Claus) and Pat Taafe taking the Cheltenham Gold Cup on the marvellous Arkle. John Surtees made history when, having won seven world titles on a motor bike, he won another in a Grand Prix racing car.

+ Two Britons leap ahead of the world and land in gold +

TO WIN one Olympic long jump was historic; for Britain to win them both was hysterical. Lynn Davies became the first Welsh athlete to win Olympic gold when he out-leaped Ralph Boston by four centimetres in a dramatic contest (and he went on to win a silver medal in the 4 x 100m relay). Davies, whose winning jump was made in a moment of calm on a gusty day, only reached the final pool with the last of his qualifying jumps. Two years later he was the first athlete ever to hold Olympic, European and Commonwealth titles at the same time, and he retained that Commonwealth long jump title in 1970.

Mary Rand's performance was even more astonishing. The first British female to win an Olympic field event, she broke the existing record with every one of her seven jumps and broke the world record with the best of them. That was not the end of her Tokyo achievements: she won the silver medal in the pentathlon and a bronze in the women's 4 x 100m relay.

Britain's outstanding all-round athlete of all time, she held the national titles in seven different events during her career.

Sensational run by Ann Packer takes Olympic title + Sen

ANN PACKER was in the Olympic team primarily as a 400-metre runner and in that event she won the silver medal. Her success in the 800m was almost unbelievable. She barely qualified for the final and surged to the front of the field with a powerful burst just 30 metres from the tape, breaking the Olympic record with a time of 2min 01.1sec.

It was only the eighth time she had ever run the distance and when the Games were over, at the age of 22, she retired and married athlete Robbie Brightwell.

+ Law rules in Europe +

DENIS LAW, Manchester United's magical forward, was in 1964 named European Footballer of the Year. Law left home in Aberdeen to join Huddersfield Town at the age of 17. Three years later he was with Manchester City, then Turin, and in 1962 back to England and United, where he spent his greatest years. He scored 30 goals for Scotland.

CHAMPIONS OF THE WORLD

Athletics
Cross-country team - England
Golf
Amateur team - Great Britain & Ireland
Motor Cycling
500cc - Mike Hailwood
250cc - Phil Read
Motocross, 500cc - Jeff Smith
Motor Racing
Grand Prix - John Surtees
Rackets
Geoffrey Atkins
Snooker
John Pulman

OLYMPIC CHAMPIONS

Athletics
20km walk - Ken Matthews
Long jump - Lynn Davies
800m, women - Ann Packer
Long jump, women - Mary Rand
Bobsleigh
Tony Nash and Robin Dixon

WORLD RECORDS

Athletics
30,000m - Jim Alder: 1hr 34min 01.8sec.
Marathon (world best) - Basil Heatley: 2hr 13min 55sec.
Marathon, women (w.b.) - Dale Greig: 3hr 27min 45sec.
Long jump, women - Mary Rand: 22ft 2in.
Motoring
Speed - Donald Campbell: 403.10 mph.
Powerboating
Speed - Donald Campbell: 276.30 mph.

1964 IS SPONSORED BY
HANSON PLC

Britain's best post-war Olympic Games successes in Track and Field events were achieved in Toyko in October 1964. Lynn Davies, Ken Matthews, Ann Packer and Mary Rand won gold medals in an outstanding British success story.

In the same year another British success story began – that of Hanson PLC. Twenty-eight years later Hanson is one of Britain's top six businesses having achieved an unbroken successful record of increases in earnings per share and dividends every year.

Hanson is an industrial management company with operating subsidiaries in the UK and the USA, principally in basic industries. Its companies enjoy leading market positions with well established brand names, employing over 80,000 people worldwide.

Hanson

In the UK Hanson's activities include Imperial Tobacco (John Player, Superkings, Regal and Embassy cigarettes), London Brick and Butterley Brick, ARC crushed stone products, Beazer Homes, Crabtree Electrical Industries and Seven Seas Health Products. The USA includes Peabody Coal, Cavenham Forest Industries, SCM Chemicals, Jacuzzi whirlpool baths and Tommy Armour golf equipment.

Hanson maintains a decentralised management structure which gives real responsibility to those in charge of its businesses and sets strong incentives for its managers to exceed realistic profit goals.

Hanson supports the British Sports Trust by sponsoring the Hanson Leadership Award within the Community Sports Leaders Award scheme. Hanson believes that good leadership is the key to success in both sport and industry.

We are proud to be associated with "Champions of the Queen – 40 glorious years of sport". The champions of 1964 certainly inspired us.

1965

LIVERPOOL had won the Football League championship in 1964 for only the second time since the war, taking them into the European Cup the following season. They reached the semi-final against Inter-Milan after an extraordinary battle with Cologne in the previous round: three drawn matches (0-0, 0-0, 2-2) had in the end to be resolved by the toss of a coin.

Liverpool won the call but lost the semi-final, but their great football machine was beginning to roll. In 25 years they captured the League title 12 times and reached seven F.A. Cup Finals, winning four, including the 1965 final against Leeds. West Ham had some joy this year too, taking the European Cup-Winners' Cup at Wembley with a 2-0 win over TSV Munich 1860.

England cricket was on a slighty bumpy path under M.J.K. Smith just now, but Dixon and Nash were still doing their stuff on the bob run, Ron Hill was slaying them in his string vest and Mr & Mrs Colclough had regained their artistic dance title on roller skates.

+ Jim Clark takes the 'Indy' as well as another world championship + Jim Clark takes

JIM CLARK, a prosperous Scottish farmer, was rated among the greatest of all Grand Prix racing drivers and briefly dominated the scene as no other man had ever done. In 1963 he set a record by winning seven Grand Prix races in one season, and in 1965 he won another six as well as the Indianapolis '500'. Between 1959 and 1968, when he was killed on the Hockenheim circuit, he won a record 61 Formula One and Formula Libre races.

Queen Marion the First +

MARION COAKES (later Marion Mould) this year won the first women's world show jumping championship on Stroller. In Mexico three years later she was to become the first woman ever to win an individual Olympic show jumping medal. After 1974 women competed equally with men in these world championships as well as in the Olympics.

Headingley boundary blitz in Test triple-ton by John Edrich

AGAINST New Zealand at Headingley, opening batsman John Edrich became only the third Englishman to score a triple century in Test matches (after Hammond and Hutton). In the course of nine innings this summer, Edrich amassed 1,311 runs. He hit 103 centuries in his first-class career, 12 of them in Test cricket, but there was never another to match this astonishing innings.

His 310 not out contained some of the most powerful lofted straight driving to which bowling had ever been subjected, a record 238 of the runs coming in boundaries – five sixes and 52 fours.

Champion Arkle runs away with Gold Cup again

ONE of the rare horses to become more famous than the jockeys who rode them, Arkle, twice National Hunt champion of the year, was the most popular and successful jumper of the 1960s. Uniquely, Arkle and Pat Taafe won the Cheltenham Gold Cup for three successive years (1964-5-6).

Out of 35 starts, the horse won 27 races and never fell, bringing home a record £75,249 to the owner, Anne, Duchess of Westminster.

CHAMPIONS OF THE WORLD

Athletics
Cross-country team - England

Bobsleigh
Tony Nash and Robin Dixon

Canoeing
Canoe sailing - Alan Emus

Cycling
Road - Tommy Simpson

Equestrianism
Show jumping, women - Marion Coakes

Motor Cycling
500cc - Mike Hailwood
250cc - Phil Read
Motocross, 500cc - Jeff Smith

Motor Racing
Grand Prix - Jim Clark

Roller Skating
Dance - Brian and Patricia Colclough

Snooker
John Pulman

Weightlifting
90kg - Louis Martin

WORLD RECORDS

Athletics
15 miles - Ron Hill: 1hr 12min 48.2sec.
25,000m - Ron Hill: 1hr 15min 22.6sec.
30,000m - Tim Johnston: 1hr 32min 34.6sec.

Gliding
300km, women - Anne Burns: 53.81 mph.
500km, women - Anne Burns: 64.16 mph.

1966

WHAT more does one need to say about 1966 other than that England won the World Cup, before a packed house at Wembley and literally countless millions of television viewers – probably 31 million at home and 400 million worldwide. Such dancing in the streets had not been seen since VE-Day. There was, though, sorrow in some quarters of the land: England were there as hosts, but no other British nation qualified for the finals.

What more? Well, Henry Cooper might like us to remember his second noble failure against Cassius Clay at another London football ground, Highbury. And Brian Close would surely like to be recorded the oddly glorious saga of the Test series with the West Indies.

After losing three and drawing one under the captaincies of first Mike Smith and then Colin Cowdrey, the selectors turned for the final Test at The Oval to the Yorkshire skipper, Close. Graveney, brought back for the series, hit 165 and England won by an innings. There were two record partnerships, 217 for the eighth wicket between Graveney and Murray (112), and a more astonishing 128 for the tenth wicket between Higgs and Snow.

England on top of the world after extra-time sensation at Wembley

ENGLAND boasted a remarkable record during these World Cup final matches. After a goalless draw against Uruguay, they conceded only one goal while beating Mexico, France, Argentina and Portugal. (The Argentine captain, Rattin, was sent off during the quarter-final at Wembley after a prolonged argument with the referee.)

In the final with West Germany (to whom they had never lost), England were 0-1 down after 13 minutes and level (through a Hurst header) at half-time. With 12 minutes to go, Peters gave England a 2-1 lead, wiped out in the last minute. It was the first final to go to extra time since 1934.

After 10 minutes a tremendous shot from Hurst bounced down from the underside of the bar. After consulting his Soviet linesman, the Swiss referee controversially awarded the goal. Any doubts about the win were forgotten when Hurst scored again with his left foot in the final minute of the match.

Hurst makes soccer history

GEOFF HURST'S first appearance for England was in a friendly against West Germany at Wembley in February, 1966. Five months later he found himself the most celebrated striker in the world as he fired in three goals against the Germans, the first hat-trick to be scored in a World Cup final. Hurst was still England's central striker when they were beaten by West Germany in the quarter-finals of the next World Cup, in Mexico.

Cooper cut again: Cassius Clay wins in sixth

HENRY COOPER was a fighter for whom even opponents found it hard not to feel some affection. At 32 this was almost certainly his last chance to take the world heavyweight title. Clay had been seriously floored, almost beaten, by one Cooper punch in 1963 and nearly all the 44,000 at Highbury Stadium were there in the hope of seeing the Londoner land another such left hook. It never came. For three rounds the Briton held his own, maybe even led. Then Clay went to town, Cooper's left eyebrow split and in the sixth, none too soon, the referee stopped the fight.

Bobby Charlton is Europe's footballer of the year

BOBBY CHARLTON of Manchester United (and no other club) remained for years England's favourite footballer. Between 1958 and 1970, he was in four World Cup squads, won a record 106 international caps and scored a record 49 goals for England. He had totalled 180 for United when he retired in 1973.

In 1966 his club, reigning League champions, reached the semi-final of the European Cup; Charlton scored both England goals in the World Cup semi-final against Portugal; and he was named European Footballer of the Year.

CHAMPIONS OF THE WORLD

Athletics
Cross-country team - England
Bowls
David Bryant
Boxing
Flyweight - Walter McGowan (WBC)
Cycling
Pursuit, women - Beryl Burton
Football
World Cup - England
Ice Skating
Dance - Bernard Ford and Diane Towler
Motor Cycling
350cc - Mike Hailwood
250cc - Mike Hailwood
Snooker
John Pulman
Amateur - Gary Owen

WORLD RECORDS

Athletics
30,000m - Jim Hogan: 1hr 32min 25.4sec.

1966 IS SPONSORED BY
THE EVENING STANDARD

A SUITABLY serious candidate for the most glorious year in the history of English sport. Grown men cried as England's soccer team, urged on by a 93,000 crowd, won the World Cup at Wembley, beating West Germany 4-2 after extra time. History will tell you that West Ham's Bobby Moore was captain and that West Ham's Geoff Hurst (three) and Martin Peters scored the goals but it was a great team triumph, from Alf Ramsey, the manager who was knighted because of the victory, to toothless Nobby Stiles and balding Bobby Charlton.

Everton won the FA Cup, defeating Sheffield Wednesday 3-2, but there was disappointment for Merseyside when League champions Liverpool fought their way through to the European Cup Winners Cup Final only to lose 2-1 to Borussia Dortmund at Hampden Park.

Evening Standard

Golf's Golden Bear came, saw and conquered. Jack Nicklaus won the Open at Muirfield – the first of his three victories – while on Wimbledon's Centre Court the fluent Manuel Santana of Spain defeated Dennis Ralston (USA) 6-4, 11-9, 6-4 and fierce Billie Jean King (USA) overpowered Maria Bueno (Brazil) 6-3, 3-6, 6-1.

There was much derring-do on the country's cricket fields. Yorkshire won the county championship as they had done on four occasions in the previous seven seasons while Essex finished second from bottom. Tom Graveney and Colin Milburn topped the batting averages but there was little joy in the Test series against Gary Sobers and his West Indians. Sobers averaged 103 in his eight innings, took 20 wickets and West Indies won three Tests, lost one and drew the other.

The Derby was won by Scobie Breasley on Charlottown but Lester Piggott romped to another jockeys' championship, nearly 100 winners ahead of Breasley.

1967

BUCKLING down to the business of scoring his first Test century against India in the first match he had played against them, Geoffrey Boycott made no mistake about it: 246 not out in England's total of 550 for four at Leeds. He was then dropped because he had taken too long over it.

England won five of the six Tests this summer (three each with India and Pakistan) under the captaincy of Close, but the selectors rapped his knuckles too, as a disciplinary measure, and reverted to Cowdrey for the winter tour of the West Indies. Close's Test career was unique: it covered 27 years, from the age of 18 to 45, but included only 22 caps. He played his final first-class match in 1982, when he was 51.

Ann Jones (formerly Ann Haydon) reached her first Wimbledon final this year, Beryl Burton took the last of her six world cycling championships, Foinavon won the Grand National and Lester Piggott was halfway through his run of eight consecutive years as champion jockey. Football fever still ran high, with Celtic winning the European Cup, and Glasgow Rangers and Leeds United reaching the finals of the Cup-Winners and the Fairs Cups.

+ Mike Hailwood races to ninth world title before he turns to cars + Mike Hailwood rac

MIKE HAILWOOD is the most successful racing motor cyclist ever produced in Britain. He began racing at the age of 17, at 20 was the youngest works driver in the world, and a year later (1961) won the first of his nine world championships, the 250cc title. During the next six years he won that championship twice more, the 350cc title twice, and the 500cc crown for four consecutive years.

In 1967 he moved from motorcycling to motor car racing, but crashed so badly in the 1974 German Grand Prix that he could not drive again. At 38, he returned to two wheels, won the Isle of Man TT again and the new Formula One world title.

+ Jonah king of squash + Jo

IN THE many years before squash instituted a world championship, the one to win was the British Open and the man who won it more often than anyone of his day was Jonah Barrington, a somewhat fanatical Cornishman.

Barrington first won the British Open in 1967 and in the next six years failed only once to become the champion. He became a pro in 1969 and was succeeded as king of the squash court by Geoff Hunt (Australia) in 1972, but Jonah remained a good enough player to win the 1980 British Closed title at the age of 39, at which stage he had not been beaten by a Briton for 15 years.

+ Celtic first British club to lift European Cup + Celtic

CELTIC football club, with Dalglish already banging in the goals, were now in a golden run of national and international success. The first British side to reach the final of the European Cup, they won it by beating Inter-Milan 2-1 in Lisbon and then faced Racing Club of Argentina, in the so-called World Club Championship.

Celtic won 1-0 in Glasgow, lost 2-1 in Buenos Aires and had to play-off in Montevideo. It was not one of football's proudest days. The Scottish goalkeeper was laid out even before the match started and by the time it ended (1-0 to Racing Club) four Celtic players and two Argentinians had been sent off.

Water-ski crown for Briton +

WATER-SKIING had seen no British world champions until this year, when at the age of 19 Jeanette Stewart-Wood won both the overall women's world championship and the jumping competition. It was 10 years before a British man equalled her achievement and she remains the only British woman to have been overall champion.

CHAMPIONS OF THE WORLD

Athletics
Cross-country team - England
Cross-country team, women - England

Billiards
Amateur - Leslie Driffield

Curling
Team - Scotland

Cycling
Road, amateur - George Webb
Road, women - Beryl Burton

Ice Skating
Dance - Bernard Ford and Diane Towler

Motor Cycling
350cc - Mike Hailwood
125cc - Bill Ivy

Rackets
Geoffrey Atkins

Tenpin Bowling
David Pond

Water Skiing
Overall, women - Jeanette Stewart-Wood
Jumps, women - Jeanette Stewart-Wood

WORLD RECORDS

Athletics
1500m, women - Anne Smith: 4min 17.3sec.
1 mile, women - Anne Smith: 4min 39.2sec.
1 mile, women - Anne Smith: 4min 37.0sec.
3 x 800m relay, women - United Kingdom: 6min 20.0sec.
3 x 880yd relay, women - United Kingdom: 6min 25.2sec.

Water Skiing
Jump, women - Jeanette Stewart-Wood: 106ft 3in. (equalled)

Bernard Ford and Diane Towler, who won the world ice dance title from 1966 to 1969, were the fifth couple in a British series who wore that crown for 15 years between 1951 and 1969.

1967 IS SPONSORED BY
BASS BREWERS

THE foundations of the great Bass brewing empire were laid by William Bass, a carrier, when he bought a small brewery in High Street, Burton-on-Trent in 1777.

The business flourished and expanded, firstly through its exports of strong ale to the Baltic states and then through brewing India Pale Ale which from the 1820s onwards was shipped in vast quantities to India and began to be popular at home too.

By the end of the 19th century Bass was established as the country's largest brewer, with three breweries, over thirty malthouses and numerous other premises. 16 miles of its own private railway line ensured swift transport of raw materials and casks. Annual output stood at over 1,000,000 barrels.

In 1875 the famous Red Triangle became the world's first registered trade mark.

Bass merged with Worthington, another Burton brewer in 1927 and famous brand names like Draught Bass and Worthington Best Bitter are still brewed today having been joined over the years by others such as Carling Black Label and the Tennents range of lagers.

Bass enters the 1990s as the UK's leading brewer but also with a wide range of interests in the hotel and leisure field internationally. The headquarters of the company, though, remain at Burton and its history and traditions are preserved at the Bass Museum in Horninglow Street where visitors can enjoy discovering how beer is brewed and also see the home of the famous Bass Shires.

1968

SEX tests by chromosome count were introduced at the Mexico Olympics, at least one result of which was a complete absence of the fearsome Press sisters. David Hemery ran out of his skin in the 400 metres hurdles and Bob Braithwaite caught the British press on the hop by winning the first shooting gold medal Britain had seen for 44 years. In the clay pigeon trench event, he scored 187 consecutive hits.

The high altitude wrecked some hopes in the long-distance running events (Africans won every men's event of more than 800 metres), but it did no harm at all to the two most famous jumpers in history, Dick Fosbury (high) and Bob Beamon (very long).

Basil d'Oliveira made his Test debut, scoring 87 not out in his first match against Australia and 158 in his second. The series was drawn, but England did come back from the West Indies with the only win in a five-match series in which the West Indians had to follow-on in two of the drawn games. And Virginia Wade, still nine years off her only Wimbledon singles final, had three wins in Britain's 4-3 victory in the Wightman Cup.

George voted the best as United sweep to their first European triumph + George voted th

GEORGE BEST was named European Footballer of the Year in 1968, the season that his club, Manchester United, won the European Cup by beating Benfica 4-1 after extra time in the Wembley final. They lost the World Club Championship 2-1 on aggregate to Estudiantes of Argentina, with Nobby Stiles sent off in the first leg and Best in the second.

Best with the ball at his feet was a magician without equal in Britain, the biggest box office draw since Stanley Matthews. The Belfast boy was signed by Manchester United at the age of 15 and was first capped by Northern Ireland when he was 18.

An eccentric and undisciplined lifestyle led to spasmodic absences (he was put on the transfer list in December 1972 and announced his retirement a fortnight later, at the age of 26) and the eventual dissolution of a genius who was perhaps the most wonderfully talented footballer in the world.

+ Finnegan hits the top +

CHRIS FINNEGAN became Britain's first boxing Olympic gold medallist for 12 years (and certainly the least expected) when he survived two standing counts in his middleweight semi-final and went on to win a split decision over Kiselyov (USSR). A bricklayer by trade, Finnegan was neither an A.B.A. nor even a divisional champion back home, but he later enjoyed a successful professional ring career.

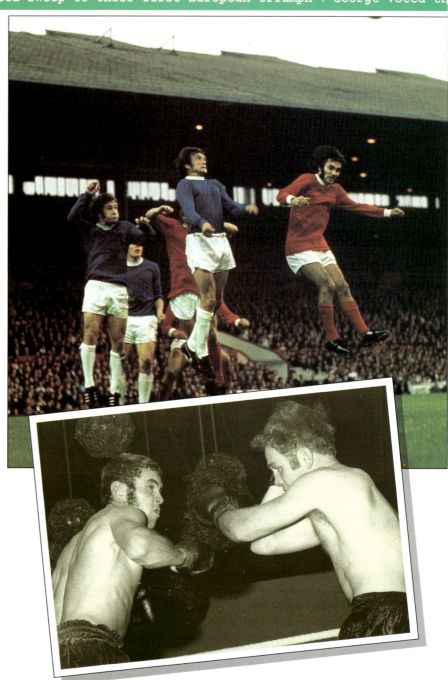

+ Hemery way ahead in historic world record run + Hemery

DAVID HEMERY'S 400-metre hurdles win in Mexico was one of the most electrifying races ever seen. It was much the fastest run of his life and he finished six metres (nine-tenths of a second) ahead of the field in a world record time.

It was the first British win in this event since Lord Burghley took the gold medal 40 years earlier and it and sent commentators into a frenzy. Britain's John Sherwood was third, well inside the previous British record – a minor triumph brushed aside in the ecstasy of Hemery's moment.

+ Olympic win for Britain's Flying Dutchman + Olympic win

FIVE first places and one second in seven races gave yachtsmen Rodney Pattisson and Iain Macdonald-Smith an overwhelming Olympic win in the Flying Dutchman class at Acapulco Bay. Their total of three penalty points in 'Superdocious' was an Olympic record.

Helmsman Pattisson, a naval officer, was going to do all this again: he won the same class at Kiel in the 1972 Games (with Chris Davies as crew). After taking four firsts and a third from the first six races, they had no need to sail in the last one.

CHAMPIONS OF THE WORLD

Athletics
Cross-country, team - England

Billiards
Rex Williams

Boxing
Featherweight - Howard Winstone (WBC)

Cycling
Pursuit - Hugh Porter

Ice Skating
Dance - Bernard Ford and Diane Towler

Motor Cycling
250cc - Phil Read
125cc - Phil Read

Motor Racing
Grand Prix - Graham Hill

Snooker
John Pulman
Amateur - David Taylor

Speedway
Team - Great Britain

OLYMPIC CHAMPIONS

Athletics
400m hurdles - David Hemery

Boxing
Middleweight - Chris Finnegan

Sailing
Flying Dutchman - Rodney Pattisson and Iain McDonald-Smith

Shooting
Trap - Bob Braithwaite

WORLD RECORDS

Athletics
400m hurdles - David Hemery: 48.1sec.
10 miles - Ron Hill: 47min 02.2sec.
10 miles - Ron Hill: 46min 44.0sec.
20 miles - Ron Hill: 1hr 36min 38sec.
4 x 110yd relay, women - United Kingdom: 45.0sec.
4 x 200m relay, women - United Kingdom: 1min 33.8sec.

SPORTS AID FOUNDATION

IN THE Summer of 1968, Britain celebrated as David Hemery scorched round the Mexico City 400m hurdle track in world record time to take Olympic gold and a place in the history books.

Having reached the peak of athletic achievement, Hemery went on to win numerous accolades, and it was his performances, along with those of our other national sporting heroes, which inspired the creation of the Sports Aid Foundation. Officially established in 1976, SAF has remained true to its aims of helping talented British sportspeople in their pursuit of sporting excellence by awarding grants to individual competitors who need help with training expenses.

SAF is a fund raising body with two arms operating nationally. SAF Limited, a non-profit making company, helps Britain's top sportspeople prepare for the Olympic, World, European and Commonwealth competitions. The SAF Charitable Trust, a registered charity, assists disabled athletes and talented youngsters to develop their full sporting potential.

Watering the grassroots of British sport are SAF's regional offices, who distribute grants to promising sportspeople in their area to offset the costs of kit and travel.

British hopes are riding high for the Barcelona Olympics, and SAF is supporting the bid for medals by awarding grants to every member of the British team who needs financial assistance to prepare for the Games.

Olympic and World Champions who have received SAF support at some time in their career include Adrian Moorhouse, Tessa Sanderson, Torvill and Dean, Richard Fox and Paralympic gold medallist, Ian Hayden, to name but a few.

As long as Britain takes pride in its sporting heroes, SAF will raise funds through commercial sponsorship, donations and events to continue "Giving Britons a Better Sporting Chance."

1969

NO QUESTION but that this was a great year for British sport. Two Wimbledon titles and the Open golf provided the cream, but there were riches beneath. Jackie Stewart won the first of his three Grand Prix motor racing championships (no Briton ever won as many) and the European titles of eventing and show jumping were won by Mary Gordon-Watson and (for the third time) David Broome.

Team sports were not far behind. Ray Illingworth replaced the injured Cowdrey as England cricket captain and had instant success, winning the two short summer Test series without losing a match. In his second game as captain he hit his highest Test score, 113 against the West Indians at Lord's. The New Zealanders followed, and were bemused by the left-arm trickery of Derek 'Deadly' Underwood: 7 for 32 in one innings at Lord's, 12 for 101 in two at The Oval.

In rugby union, South Africa toured the UK for the last time, drawing with Ireland and Wales and losing to Scotland and England in an atmosphere of intense hostility. England's soccer team were on a high too, winning seven of their 10 internationals and losing only one, 1-2 in Brazil.

+ Post-war history made as Ann Jones enjoys double triumph at Wimbledon + Post-war

ANN JONES this year became the only British tennis player since the war to win two titles at Wimbledon. Her singles battle with Billie Jean King showed the remarkable tenacity of the Briton. She not only reversed her defeat by the same player in the 1967 final, but was only the second woman in 45 years to win the title after losing the first set. The following day she won the mixed doubles with Fred Stolle.

Ann Jones, whose real name is Adrianne, reached the Wimbledon quarter-finals nine times and played 32 Wightman Cup rubbers. Her tennis successes caused the public to forget that she had been one of the world's outstanding exponents of table tennis. The daughter of two international players, she was capped for England (as Ann Haydon) at the age of 15 and reached the world singles final five times.

Women pass the Test + Wome

WOMEN had been playing Test cricket since 1934, but this year well illustrated the scope and seriousness of their activity. England had a four-month, six-Test tour of Australia and New Zealand (two wins, four draws) during which two batsmen (Audrey Didsbury and Rachel Hayhoe) scored more than 1,000 runs and Enid Bakewell achieved a rare tour double: 1,031 runs at an average of 39.6 and 118 wickets at 9.7. In one match against New South Wales, wicket-keeper Shirley Hodges stumped eight batsmen and conceded no byes.

Tony Jacklin drives to the top and golf glory at The Open

TONY JACKLIN was the first Briton to win golf's greatest prize, The Open Championship, since Max Faulkner in 1951. His triumph at Lytham St Anne's (his 68-70-70-72 left him two strokes ahead of Bob Charles) proved to be of great significance for the future of British golf. He won the US Open the next year, the only Briton since 1900 to achieve that double.

Later in 1969 Jacklin won four and halved two of his Ryder Cup games at Royal Birkdale, culminating in an 18th-hole nail-biter with Jack Nicklaus in which Jacklin needed a two-foot putt to halve the game and the entire match, and Nicklaus conceded it. After being appointed non-playing Ryder Cup captain in 1983, Jacklin led the Britain and Europe team to two wins and a draw in four years.

Board thriller in Athens

LILLIAN BOARD was a uniquely tragic and much-loved figure in British athletics. Robbed of her expected 400-metre Olympic victory at almost the final stride in 1968, she was the heroine in 1969 of what was described as 'the most thrilling race ever witnessed in the 45 years of women's athletics'.

Having won the European 800m championship in Athens, she took over the last leg of the 4 x 400m relay just behind the girl who had beaten her in Mexico, Colette Bresson of France. With 200m to go, Board was a full eight metres down. Defying the impossible, she broke the tape with inches to spare in a new world record time.

Despite a brave and highly-publicised fight, Lillian Board was felled by disease at an appallingly early age. She did not make it to the Munich Olympics of 1972, the Games at which she was likely to have proved herself the greatest female runner of her time.

CHAMPIONS OF THE WORLD

Angling
Freshwater - Robin Harris

Athletics
Cross-country team - England

Billiards
Amateur - Jack Karnehm

Canoeing
Canoe sailing - Alan Emus

Ice Skating
Dance - Bernard Ford and Diane Towler

Lacrosse
Women - Great Britain

Motor Cycling
125cc - Dave Simmonds

Motor Racing
Grand Prix - Jackie Stewart

Roller Skating
10,000m - John Folley

Snooker
John Spencer

WORLD RECORDS

Athletics
4 x 400m relay, women - United Kingdom: 3min 37.6sec.
4 x 400m relay, women - United Kingdom: 3min 30.8sec.

1970

SCOTLAND staged the Commonwealth Games for the first time, and for the first time Kenyan runners began to dominate middle distances. Not the 3000 metres, where Ian Stewart had a superb run to leave Kip Keino in the shade with another Scot, Ian McCafferty, second. A third, Lachie Stewart, won the 10,000 metres.

Britain's female athletes continued their habit of breaking relay records every year, following the 1969 400-metre stunner with a new 4 x 800m time. Mary Gordon-Watson on Cornishman became the first Briton to win the world three-day event crown, Tony Jacklin rose to absurd heights in the US Open and Henry Cooper regained the British title that he had voluntarily relinquished the previous year.

After the political collapse of the South African cricket tour to England, a strong replacement was found in a 'Rest of the World' side, which won four of the five Tests. Strongest horse of the flat season was surely the wondrous Nijinsky, which this season won the classic treble of 2000 Guineas, Derby and St. Leger (all with Piggott up) as well as the Irish Derby, and finished the season with record prize money of £159,681.

Broome orchestrates first world championship win for Britain and Beethoven + Broome

DAVID BROOME had already been an international show jumping success for 10 years when he won the 1970 world championships on Beethoven, and he was still riding for Britain in the Olympics 18 years after that. On Sunsalve he won an Olympic individual bronze in 1960 and the European championship in 1961. On Mister Softee he took two more European titles (1967 and 1969) and his second Olympic bronze (1968).

He was national champion six times between 1961 and 1986, and his world title was the first (and so far the only one) by a British rider.

Jacklin storms to US Open

TONY JACKLIN was the first Briton to win the US Open golf championship for 50 years, and only the third in history. He was under par every round, putted no more than 113 times over the 72 holes and won by a stunning seven strokes.

Porter successfully pursues world track championship

HUGH PORTER was one of the few track cyclists of world class to emerge in Britain since the war. Individual pursuit was his speciality, and as an amateur he won a bronze medal in the 1963 world championships and a gold in the 1966 Commonwealth Games. After turning pro, he became world champion in 1968, 1970, 1972 and 1973. He married Olympic swimming gold medallist Anita Lonsbrough.

Fencing record for Briton

BILL HOSKYNS competed in six Olympic Games, a record for any British sportsman. Probably the greatest, and certainly the most durable, of all the nation's fencers, he was the world epee champion in 1958 and runner-up in 1965; and in the Olympics won team silver in 1960 and individual silver in 1964.

A Somerset farmer by trade, he was in this year of 1970 Commonwealth Games epee champion for the fourth successive time. His career total of nine Commonwealth Games gold medals included one for sabre.

CHAMPIONS OF THE WORLD

Athletics
Cross-country - Michael Tagg
Cross-country team - England
Cross-country team, women - England
Caber-tossing - Arthur Rowe

Boxing
Lightweight - Ken Buchanan (WBA)

Cycling
Pursuit - Hugh Porter

Equestrianism
Show jumping - David Broome
Three-day eventing - Mary Gordon-Watson
Three-day eventing, team - United Kingdom

Motor Cycling
250cc - Rod Gould

Rackets
Geoffrey Atkins

Snooker
Ray Reardon
Amateur - Jonathan Barron

WORLD RECORDS

Athletics
30,000m - Jim Alder: 1hr 31min 30.4sec.
Marathon (world best) - Ron Hill: 2hr 9min 28sec.
4 x 800m relay, women - United Kingdom: 8min 27.0sec.
4 x 800m relay, women - United Kingdom: 8min 25.0sec.

MINISTERS FOR SPORT

THE first Minister with special responsibility for sport appointed by the Government was Lord Hailsham, in December 1962. He was then Lord President of the Council and Minister for Science. The following Labour Government established an advisory Sports Council, which became an independent body with a Royal Charter in 1972.

After the Conservative Government had been returned to power in 1992, no Minister for sport was named. Responsibility for sport (and for the arts, broadcasting and tourism) passed to a new Heritage department headed by a Cabinet Minister, David Mellor.

GOVERNMENT MINISTERS WITH RESPONSIBILITY FOR SPORT

1962   LORD HAILSHAM
1964   DENIS HOWELL
1970   ELDON GRIFFITHS
1974   DENIS HOWELL
1979   HECTOR MUNRO
1981   NEIL MCFARLANE
1985   RICHARD TRACEY
1987   COLIN MOYNIHAN
1990   ROBERT ATKINS

Denis Howell

Colin Moynihan

1971

EVEN apart from glamorous Arsenal's 'double', this was a triumphant year for football. With both Banks and Shilton available in goal, England remained unbeaten in their nine matches, scoring 19 goals to four. Chelsea won the European Cup-Winners' Cup in a replay with Real Madrid and Leeds won the Fairs Cup on away goals after two draws with Juventus.

Ray Illingworth's England cricketers not only regained the Ashes in Australia (the first time since 1888 that the Aussies had failed to win a single match in a Test series at home), but beat both New Zealand (Underwood 6 for 12 in 12 overs in the first Test) and Pakistan.

Britain's horsewomen were riding high again, with Ann Moore winning the first of her two European show jumping titles on Psalm and Princess Anne taking the eventing crown. On two feet, David Bedford opened international eyes with his world cross-country win, Joyce Smith moved into world class with a record at 3,000 metres (she later ran to greater glory in marathons) and young David Jenkins became European champion at 400 metres.

mph + Barry John humbles All-Blacks in British Lions' historic tour triumph + Barry

BARRY JOHN was the greatest fly-half of his time and among the greatest of all time. He first played for Wales at the age of 21, and by the time he retired less than six years later had scored 90 points for his country in 25 games. He scored more than twice as many in one glorious tour with the British Lions in 1971, after Wales had won the Grand Slam.

Against the All-Blacks, the Lions won two of the four Tests and drew one, as well as winning all the other matches of the tour. It was the first time the Lions had ever won a series in New Zealand.

+ Skipper sees it through

RAY ILLINGWORTH'S unexpected tenure of the England captaincy was refreshing for its no-nonsense approach. His finest hour, no doubt, was in Melbourne early this year when he regained the Ashes that had been held by Australia since 1959.

At the end of a long and difficult tour, England were without Boycott for the seventh Test in Sydney; were taken off the field by their captain on the second day under a rain of beer cans; and lost Snow (whose 7 for 40 won the fourth Test) early in Australia's second innings.

Princess Anne crowned head of Europe's event riders

PRINCESS ANNE had her first major success when, riding Doublet, she won the European three-day event championship at Burghley. It was a surprise even to the experts, and clearly to the team from the Soviet Union, whose eyes widened as this fairy tale came true. They had completed the course in some exhaustion when in galloped this real and lively young princess.

It was to the Soviet Union that Princess Anne went in 1973 to defend her title, this time with Goodwill, but before the massed ranks of the world's press she came to grief (as many others did) at Kiev's horrific second obstacle.

+ Arsenal on the double +

ARSENAL had not won the F.A. Cup for 21 years, nor the League championship for 18, when they did the 'double' this season, for the first time in their history. Though the team did not boast outstanding stars, manager Bertie Mee was able to field eight international footballers in the Cup Final who had between them, significantly, played more than 1,500 times for the club. They had won the European Fairs Cup the previous season and reached the F.A. Cup Final again in 1972.

CHAMPIONS OF THE WORLD

Archery
Field, women - Barbara Fielding
Athletics
Cross-country - David Bedford
Cross-country team - England
Cross-country team, women - England
Billiards
Leslie Driffield
Amateur - Norman Dagley
Motor Cycling
250cc - Phil Read
Motor Racing
Grand Prix - Jackie Stewart
Powerlifting
67.5kg - Michael Shaw
Snooker
John Spencer
Speedway
Team - Great Britain

WORLD RECORDS

Athletics
400m hurdles, women - Sandra Dyson: 61.1sec.
3,000m, women - Joyce Smith: 9min 23.4sec.

> MOHAMMED ALI in March lost his first world heavyweight fight for seven years. He was beaten for the title by Joe Frazier, but regained it three years later by beating George Foreman in Zaire.

1971 IS SPONSORED BY

BRITISH NUCLEAR FUELS plc

IN THE 21 years since the formation of British Nuclear Fuels plc, the Company has shown a considerable commitment to sport particularly at the amateur level.

The principal benefactor has been athletics. BNFL made the major financial contribution to the construction of a magnificent new stadium in West Cumbria near to the town of Whitehaven. This facility, which is the home of the successful Copeland Athletics Club, has been the venue for a number of high quality events attracting competitors worldwide. This year BNFL will be sponsoring the annual British Under 23 Home International at the Stadium bringing the Company's total contribution to the sport over the last few years to almost £1.5 million.

The Company has also taken a special interest in Rugby League; a sport which carries considerable popularity in the areas surrounding its main plants.

The British Amateur Rugby League Challenge Cup has been sponsored by BNFL for the last three years. This is the most popular Rugby League competition in the world, attracting well over two hundred entries from teams covering virtually all areas of England and Wales. Additionally significant donations have been made to the amateur game at both county and Club level within Cumbria.

Professional Rugby League has also benefitted through sponsorship of the Cumbria County, Whitehaven and Workington Town clubs amounting to almost £250,000 over the last six years.

Perhaps the most striking has been the breadth of sports covered by the company's policy of support through sponsorship or direct donation to clubs and recreational bodies within West Cumbria. Almost every sporting organisation operating within the area has gained from this including nationally recognised activities such as angling, horse riding through to golf and locally traditional sports such as hound trailing, Cumberland and Westmorland Wrestling and fell racing.

Overall, BNFL has donated some £2 million to sport since its inauguration in 1971. It is not, however, only the recipient organisation who have benefited. The Company has in return gained considerable goodwill particularly from its association with amateur activities. Not least in the reasons for this is the fact that the participants are enmeshed in the very fabric of the community.

1972

IT IS hard to remember the Munich Olympics without pain, but behind it lay some glorious performances. There was Olga Korbut, who opened the door to the world of gymnastics, and Mark Spitz, whose seven swimming gold medals were an Olympic record. There were the all-conquering women of East Germany and the first Olympic women's 1500 metres (12 years later they were running the marathon). And there were three individual gold medals for Britain, two of them won by 33-year-old competitors.

Mary Peters of Belfast was the one never to be forgotten, hurling herself over that pentathlon high bar in the darkness of the summer night; but horseman Richard Meade won his third Olympic gold in Munich, and yachtsman Rodney Pattisson (in Kiel) his second. On the sidelines was Britain's dressage expert, Lorna Johnstone, who was the oldest woman ever to compete in the Olympics when she was placed 12th five days after her 70th birthday.

There was success elsewhere too: Britain's carriage drivers won the world championship for the first time; Virginia Wade won the US Open tennis title; and Tony Jacklin would have won the Open golf again had he sunk a putt from 15 feet.

ich + Ireland's golden girl rises to the greatest of her triumphs in Munich + Ireland

MARY PETERS, the greatest all-round athlete in the history of Northern Ireland, set a world record when she won the Olympic pentathlon with 4,801 points. These were her third Games (she was fourth in 1964), and in the Commonwealth Games of 1970 she had won both the pentathlon and the shot put.

Her Munich performance was positively heroic, and by her subsequent devotion to the encouragement of athletics in Belfast she remained a golden figure long after her retirement from competition.

Derby record equalled + De

LESTER PIGGOTT rode his sixth Derby winner, bringing Roberto home to equal Jem Robinson's record of the early 19th century. Then 35 years old, Piggott was still to be riding 20 years later (after a little break) and took his Derby triumphs to nine. The first of them was Never Say Die, at odds of 33-1, when Piggott was only 18.

He rode 191 winners in 1966 and was champion flat jockey 11 times in all, including the eight years from 1964 to 1971. (Sir Gordon Richards, his greatest predecessor, was champion 26 times.)

Britain's top Olympic rider wins two more gold medals

RICHARD MEADE contested three Olympic Games as a three-day event rider. He was fourth individual in Mexico (where Britain won the team gold medal), first in Munich (another team gold) and fourth in Montreal; and shared in the team gold medal at the 1970 world championships. All these successes were achieved on different horses, an unmistakeable sign of a great rider.

Youngest winner for snooker

ALEX HIGGINS became the youngest world champion in the history of snooker when, aged 23, he beat John Spencer by 37 frames to 32 in the final at a British Legion hall on the outskirts of Birmingham. The entrance fees provided the prize money. Though he won the title 10 years later, his aggressive nature and unstable personality caused him to be banned by his professional association in 1990.

CHAMPIONS OF THE WORLD

Athletics
Cross-country, women - Joyce Smith
Cross-country team - England
Cross-country team, women - England

Billiards
Rex Williams

Bowls
Mal Evans
Fours - England
Team - Scotland

Cycling
Pursuit - Hugh Porter

Equestrianism
Carriage driving, team - Great Britain

Powerlifting
75kg - Ronald Collins

Rugby League
World Cup - Great Britain

Snooker
Alex Higgins
Amateur - Ray Edmonds

Speedway
Pairs - Terry Betts and Ray Wilson
Team - Great Britain

Trampolining
Paul Luxon
Synchro - Paul Luxon and Robert Hughes

OLYMPIC CHAMPIONS

Athletics
Pentathlon, women - Mary Peters

Sailing
Flying Dutchman - Rodney Pattisson and Chris Davies

Show Jumping
Individual - Richard Meade
Team - United Kingdom

WORLD RECORDS

Athletics
Pentathlon, women - Mary Peters: 4,801pt.

Shooting
Small bore, prone - John Palin 600/600

1972 IS SPONSORED BY
THE SPORTS COUNCIL

1972 will inevitably, and sadly, be remembered for the "Black September" terrorist attack during the XXth Olympic Games in Munich. However, even this outrage could not totally overshadow the outstanding athletic achievements, not least the gold medals won by Mary Peters in the Pentathlon on her third Games appearance; Richard Meade in both the individual and (with Mark Phillips, Mary Gordon-Watson and Bridget Parker) the Three-Day Equestrian events; and by Rodney Pattison and Christopher Davies in the Yachting, Flying Dutchman class. Wimbledon saw Stan Smith and Billy Jean King take the titles; while the championships in English League soccer and County cricket went to Derby County and Warwickshire.

However, 1972 was also a significant year in British sporting administration. On 4 February 1972 the Royal Charter was signed establishing the GB Sports Council as the primary executive authority for sports development. Its first Chairman was Dr Roger Bannister, and Walter Winterbottom was its first Director General.

Sport changed in many ways in the ensuing years, not invariably for the better. The pressures of commerce and the media, and the growing use by too many competitors of performance-enhancing drugs, required sports administrators to learn new skills while simultaneously striving to re-assert traditional values.

It is therefore, salutary to recall that 1972 also witnessed the death of Phyllis Colson, the inspiration behind the CCPR since 1935. The steady improvement in public participation in active recreation over the years is a glowing testimony to her pioneering achievements.

1973

HAVING been skittled by an unknown Australian bowler (Bob Massie) the previous year, England felt the full force of the West Indian batsmen this summer: in their five innings of the three-match series they averaged around 400, and at Lord's hit 652 for 8 – the highest total there since 1939. So look elsewhere for British success and light instantly on David Wilkie, who was later to prove Britain's most successful male swimmer of the century.

At the first world championships, in Belgrade, he finished fourth in the 100 metres breaststroke, third in the 200m medley (in a Commonwealth record) and first in the 200m breaststroke, breaking the world record. Racing driver Jackie Stewart was another to finish first, for the third time in five years and for the last time. Liverpool finished first in the Football League, and not for the last time (10 more wins in the next 17 years) and also won the European Fairs Cup.

At Wimbledon there were some strange names on the champions' board, for this was the year the professionals went on strike. Jan Kodes beat Alex Metreveli in the men's final.

+ Brendan Foster captures world record as he moves up the running scale + Brendan

BRENDAN FOSTER was in the process of moving up the running distance scale when, in August at Crystal Palace, he broke Lasse Viren's world record for the two miles. Spectators were not aware of this for some time, nor was Foster himself. His winning time had been announced as 8min. 14.2sec., one-fifth of a second outside the record. But these were still the days when hand-held timing was the norm, and it was not until half an hour later, when the judges has studied the photo-finish of the race, that they saw the electrical time recorded as 8:13.68. Even under the rounding-up procedure, it came out at 8:13.8.

Foster had by then won 1500-metre bronze medals at both the Commonwealth Games (1970) and the European championships (1971), and two weeks after the Crystal Palace record he won the European Cup 5000m, leaving Viren in fifth place. (Britain's four other track wins at that final included one for Alan Pascoe in the 400m hurdles, in his first season at that event.)

The following year Foster's 5000m runs brought him silver at the Commonwealth Games and gold at the European Championships, but his happiest run of the year was the world record 3000m at his home track in Gateshead, where he was the local council's sport and recreation officer. By the time the Montreal Olympics came up, he was running for Britain in both 5000m (fifth) and the 10,000m (bronze medal).

+ Stewart completes his hat-trick and calls it a Grand Prix day + Stewart complet

JACKIE STEWART'S three Formula One world championship triumphs in five years are more than any other British racing driver has ever accomplished. Third in his first season of Grand Prix racing (1965), he was second in 1968, winning three races despite a broken wrist. He won the championship again in 1969 and 1971, was second in 1972 and after his third win in 1973 retired intact at the age of 34 to pursue a profitable commercial career.

+ Red Rum fastest ever + R

RED RUM and the Grand National are inseparable. It is the only horse to win the race three times, in 1973, '74 and '77, and on the other two occasions it ran (1975 and '76) it was second. In 1973, when the horse was eight years old, Brian Fletcher rode it to the fastest time ever recorded for the race, at an average speed of nearly 30 mph.

Read inches ahead of Agostini + R

PHIL READ won the first of his seven world titles on a 250cc motor bike in 1964 and the last on a 500cc 10 years later, when he was 35. In 1973 he took his first 500cc championship, after four Grand Prix wins. He secured that 'King of Speed' crown when in Sweden he beat by inches his MV Agusta teammate Giacomo Agostini, who had held the 500cc title for seven years.

Read was in the first season of a full works contract with MV, who had signed him specifically to help Agostini retain the title.

CHAMPIONS OF THE WORLD

Athletics
Cross-country team, women - England

Billiards
Rex Williams

Cricket
World Cup, women - England

Motor Cycling
500cc - Phil Read
750cc - Barry Sheene

Motor Racing
Grand Prix - Jackie Stewart
Kart, 100cc - Terry Fullerton

Powerlifting
75kg - Ronald Collins

Rackets
Howard Angus

Snooker
Ray Reardon

Speedway
Team - Great Britain

Swimming
200m breaststroke - David Wilkie

WORLD RECORDS

Athletics
2 miles - Brendan Foster: 8min 13.8sec.
10,000m - David Bedford: 27min 30.8sec.
400m hurdles, women - Judy Vernon: 60.4sec.

Swimming
200m breaststroke - David Wilkie:
 2min 19.28sec.

1974

ANABOLIC steroids were this year added to the list of substances banned by the International Olympic Committee, but at the European athletics championships they were untroubled by such decisions. Brendan Foster (5000 metres), Alan Pascoe (400m hurdles) and marathon runner Ian Thompson had the best wins of their careers. So too did Britain's Wightman Cup team, with a record 6-1 walloping of the United States at Deeside.

Rugby's unbeaten British Lions, led by Bill McBride, were the first touring team to win a Test series in South Africa since 1896, and in other matches Alan Old scored 37 points in a 97-0 win over South-West Districts. Matters were proceeding less smoothly with the round ball: Scotland were the only British nation to qualify for the World Cup finals. After draws against Brazil and Yugoslavia and a 2-0 win over Zaire they were eliminated.

Zaire, not a familiar spot on the map to most of us, was the unexpected scene of Mohammed Ali regaining the world heavyweight crown that he had lost to Joe Frazier, who had been beaten by George Foreman. Ali put Foreman away in the eighth round of 'the rumble in the jungle'.

+ JPR tests South Africa +

J.P.R. WILLIAMS was one of rugby union's most exciting players, the attacking full-back from Wales who played in all the British Lions Tests on their triumphant tour of South Africa (played 22, won 21, drawn one). Since he rarely took place kicks, he was not a high-scoring player, but he was certainly one of the first any captain would want on his side. His enthusiasm for the heat of the game was such that he would often pile in with the forwards and his immense value was reflected by the desperation with which any opposition would try to stifle him.

Double triple for Gilks + Dou

GILLIAN GILKS was Britain's supreme badminton player of her time. This year she was triple champion (singles, women's doubles and mixed doubles) of both Europe and the Commonwealth, an unprecedented achievement.

Even greater glory awaited her when in 1976 she became triple champion at the All-England tournament, the Wimbledon of her game, and repeated her European triumph. In her career, Gilks (who first played for England at the age of 16 and was still an international champion at 34) won a total of eight European and 10 All-England titles.

Test + Tony Greig destroys West Indies in final Test +

TONY GREIG had a sensational all-round series in the West Indies early this year, scoring 430 runs and taking 24 wickets in Test matches. Born in South Africa to a Scottish father, he became the first England player to score a century and take five wickets in the same innings of any Test match.

Greig virtually won the final Test for England, taking 8 for 86 and 5 for 70 with quick off-spinners. He became an invigorating captain of England in 1975, but after 14 Tests was dismissed because of his clandestine involvement with Kerry Packer and World Series Cricket.

Conteh captures world crown +

JOHN CONTEH, slick and stylish, was a glittering star of the British boxing scene. He won the world light-heavyweight title in October at his first attempt, beating Jorge Ahumada on points. He successfully defended the crown three times in the next two-and-a-half years, before losing on points in Belgrade to Mate Parlov.

CHAMPIONS OF THE WORLD

Athletics
Cross-country team, women - England
Billiards
Rex Williams
Boxing
Light-heavyweight - John Conteh (WBC)
Equestrianism
Carriage driving, team - Great Britain
Motor Cycling
500cc - Phil Read
Powerlifting
75kg - Ronald Collins
Snooker
Ray Reardon
Amateur - Ray Edmonds
Speedway
Team - England

WORLD RECORDS

Athletics
3,000m - Brendan Foster: 7min 35.2sec.
60m, women - Andrea Lynch: 7.2sec.
Swimming
200m individual medley - David Wilkie: 2min 06.32sec.

1974 IS SPONSORED BY
CARLSBERG

1974 was a year of great significance for Carlsberg.

It marked the opening of the 100-acre Bridge Street Brewery in Northampton – a brewery that today produces more than 500 million pints of lager each year.

The key factors in creating and sustaining such demand is product quality supported by high profile marketing.

Carlsberg's commitment to brewing quality is world famous and their advertising copy of 'Probably the best lager in the world' is equally well known.

The advertising is complemented by a comprehensive range of sports sponsorships which generate media coverage, positive image associations and appeal to the company's target market.

In 1974 sports sponsorship was still in its infancy, since then the medium has developed significantly and expenditure increased tenfold.

Throughout that time Carlsberg has been a very active sponsor of sport both in the UK and around the world. This year (1992) Carlsberg sponsor the British Olympic Team and the European Football Championship in Sweden.

The football theme continues when the new season commences as Carlsberg begin a four-year sponsorship of Liverpool Football Club. In 1974 Liverpool won the FA Cup and Leeds won the Championship – who said lightning doesn't strike twice!. 1974 also saw the Pakistan Cricket Team touring as they do again this year.

Sport continues to thrive and this is aided in no small way by the support of sponsors.

Carlsberg is committed to building long-term relationships with its sporting partners be it Basketball or Liverpool, European Football or Waterskiing to ensure a higher profile and real benefits for all.

1975

IT WAS 50 years since the last time Great Britain won the Wightman Cup in successive years: 6-1 in North Wales in 1974, 5-2 in America this time. Virginia Wade, Sue Barker and Glynis Coles played the singles again, but there was an interesting change in the doubles: Ann Jones was brought back, five years after retirement, to partner Wade. The two defeats were by Chris Evert, who at 19 had won Wimbledon the previous year.

Cricket staged the first one-day World Cup tournament, with the West Indies beating Australia in the final after a brilliant first-round recovery against Pakistan. In the winter England had lost the Ashes to a Lillee and Thomson bombardment, during which captain Mike Denness dropped himself from the fifth Test and in the sixth hit 188, the highest score ever made by an England skipper in Australia.

We played them again in the summer, when the captaincy passed to Greig. Gooch made his debut with two ducks in the first Test, the third was abandoned after the Leeds pitch was vandalised and the fourth was drawn after six days that opened with a first innings aggregate from the two sides of 1,070 runs.

Wilkie emerges as Britain's greatest: two world titles and three American

DAVID WILKIE was probably the greatest performer in the history of British men's swimming. He won his first world championship (200m breaststroke) in September 1973 and from that moment to the day he retired three years later was never beaten at that distance. In 1974 he won two gold medals at both the Commonwealth Games and the European championships, but in the next two years he exceeded even that.

At the world championships in Colombia in 1975 he took both the 100 and 200m breaststroke titles, then returned to his studies in Miami. At the American championships, the first Briton ever to win a title, he won both breaststroke events and the 4 x 50m individual medley.

The next year in Montreal he finished second in the 100m breaststroke to John Hencken (who broke the world record every time he swam), and then took the Olympic 200m gold in a time that beat Hencken by more than two seconds and the world record by more than three.

Big lift for Briton

POWERLIFTING was a matter of very slight public concern at this time, which accounts for the anonymity of one of Britain's most successful sportsmen. Ronald Collins won eight successive world championships, from 1972 to 1979 – three at 75kg and five at 82.5kg.

Prior-Palmer and Princess Anne take top two places in European championships

LUCINDA PRIOR-PALMER continued Britain's magnificent tradition of three-day event riding (particularly by women) when she took the European championships on Be Fair (with Princess Anne second on Goodwill). Prior-Palmer retained the title two years later on George and rode yet another horse, Regal Realm, when she won the 1982 world championships under her married name of Lucinda Green.

She won Badminton a record six times on six different horses between 1973 and 1984, and has since become one of television's best equestrian commentators.

Londoner wins in Mexico

JOHN H. STRACEY, a London East Ender, took the world welterweight boxing title in Mexico City when he ended the long run of the great Cuban, Jose Napoles. The referee stopped the fight in the sixth round. The following year Stracey defended successfully once, but lost to Carlos Palomino.

All pull together

SIX times an Olympic sport, tug-of-war staged its first world championships this year. English teams (Sheen Farmers from Staffordshire and Wood Treatment from Cheshire) won both the weight categories.

CHAMPIONS OF THE WORLD

Angling
Freshwater - Ian Heaps

Athletics
Cross-country - Ian Stewart

Billiards
Rex Williams
Amateur - Norman Dagley

Boxing
Welterweight - John H. Stracey (WBC)

Canoeing
Wildwater team, women - Great Britain

Hockey
Team, women - England

Karate
Team - Great Britain

Powerlifting
82.5kg - Ronald Collins

Snooker
Ray Reardon

Speedway
Team - England

Squash
Amateur team - Great Britain

Swimming
100m breaststroke - David Wilkie
200m breaststroke - David Wilkie

Tenpin Bowling
Doubles - Great Britain

Tug of War
720kg - England
640kg - England

1976

AN OLYMPIC boycott by African nations marred the Montreal Games, which also suffered the Onischenko fencing scandal. A British modern pentathlete, Jim Fox, exposed the cheating of his Soviet opponent, who had electrically rigged his foil to signal a hit when there was not one. The Soviets were disqualified and the Britons went on to a fairytale team victory.

There were sensational Olympic performances too by David Wilkie and John Curry, as well as by the Tornado sailors. On the unexpected front there was not much to beat the two world championship gold medals of sprint canoeist Jeremy West, nor George Lee's win in the gliding championships (his first of three).

Among the motor bike riders of the day Barry Sheene came up with his first 500cc world title and Peter Collins brought the individual speedway title back to Britain after 14 years. On quieter tracks Steve Ovett was beginning to make himself felt across the world and the great John Francome had the first of his seven years as champion National Hunt jockey.

+ Curry first-ever Briton to lift the triple crown of men's ice skating + Curry fir

JOHN CURRY, most graceful of all ice skaters, was in 1976 the first British man for 37 years to win a solo figure skating world championship, and the first ever to win a solo Olympic gold medal. In the space of only 50 days, he won the European, Olympic and world championships. He not only turned the heads of the public (largely through television) towards a sport that had been ignored, but also did much to reshape the whole presentation of figure skating by its exponents.

Angus the real champion +

FORMERLY the world rackets champion, Howard Angus took the world real tennis title in 1976 and was seldom beaten for the rest of the decade. His record compares with the greatest players of all time: world champion 1976-81, British Open champion 1970-1981 and British amateur champion for a ridiculous 16 years. A small but immensely tough left-hander, his devastating service was probably unrivalled.

+ Third place in Fuji brings Hunt first prize +

JAMES HUNT's six Grand Prix wins in 1976 have been exceeded only by Jim Clark's seven in 1963, and Hunt's total of 69 points were the next highest to Jackie Stewart's 71 in 1973. He secured his drivers' championship when he finished third at the first-ever Japanese Grand Prix. Niki Lauda, the reigning champion, had returned to the circuit after his appalling accident at the Nurburgring but withdrew from the race because of the dangerous conditions.

Hunt had three wins in 1977 and retired from the Grand Prix circuit two years later. His fluency as television's trackside expert ensured his subsequent success.

CHAMPIONS OF THE WORLD

Billiards
Rex Williams

Canoeing
500m K1 - Jeremy West
1000m K1 - Jeremy West

Golf
Amateur team - Great Britain and Ireland

Gliding
Open - George Lee

Motor Cycling
500cc - Barry Sheene

Motor Racing
Grand Prix - James Hunt

Powerlifting
100kg - Paul Jordan
82.5kg - Ronald Collins
75kg - William West
60kg - Edward Pengelly

Real Tennis
Howard Angus

Snooker
Ray Reardon
Amateur - Doug Mountjoy

Speedway
Peter Collins
Pairs - John Louis and Malcolm Simmons

Squash
Team, men - Great Britain

Tug of War
720kg - England
640kg - England

OLYMPIC CHAMPIONS

Ice Skating
John Curry

Modern Pentathlon
Team - United Kingdom

Sailing
Tornado - John Osborn and Reg White

Swimming
200m breaststroke - David Wilkie

WORLD RECORDS

Swimming
200m breaststroke - David Wilkie:
  2min 15.11sec.

+ British team in triumph

CINDERELLA went to the ball at Montreal and came back with a sackful of glass slippers. Surely no British team win in Olympic history has caused a more emotional response than that of the modern pentathletes, a penniless lot in a penniless sport that demands extraordinary commitment. Though the everlasting Jim Fox had been close to an individual medal at the Munich Olympics (one bullet one millimetre closer to the bull would have done it), this was the sport's first major international success.

It was clinched by great cross-country running on the last day from the team of Adrian Parker, Danny Nightingale and Fox *(above)*. Fox in particular showed remarkable determination in overcoming the emotional trauma of the Onischenko fencing scandal, in which he had played a leading part.

SPORTS WRITERS' ASSOCIATION

SWA

THE Sports Writers' Association of Great Britain was founded in 1948. Since 1951 the membership (now approaching 600) have elected by ballot the nation's Sportsman of the Year, who is the man thought to have brought the greatest international prestige to British sport. In 1959 a poll for the Sportswoman of the Year was added, and in 1970 for the Sports Team.

SPORTSMAN OF THE YEAR

1952 Len Hutton
1953 Gordon Pirie
1954 Roger Bannister
1955 John Disley
1956 Chris Brasher
1957 Derek Ibbotson
1958 Ian Black
1959 John Surtees
1960 Don Thompson
1961 Terry Downes
1962 Brian Kilby
1963 Jim Clark
1964 Lynn Davies
1965 Tommy Simpson
1966 England World Cup XI
1967 Mike Hailwood
1968 David Hemery
1969 Tony Jacklin
1970 Tony Jacklin
1971 Ken Buchanan
1972 Richard Meade
1973 Jackie Stewart
1974 John Conteh
1975 David Wilkie
1976 James Hunt
1977 Barry Sheene
1978 Daley Thompson
1979 Sebastian Coe
1980 Sebastian Coe
1981 Sebastian Coe
1982 Daley Thompson
1983 Steve Cram
1984 Sebastian Coe
1985 Steve Cram
1986 Lloyd Honeyghan
1987 Nick Faldo
1988 Sandy Lyle
1989 Nick Faldo
1990 Nick Faldo
1991 Kriss Akabusi

1977

TWENTY-FIVE years into the Queen's reign and we had both Jubilee and jubilation. England regained the Ashes with a 3-0 win against Australia. It was a series that saw England's first victorious Test at home for 14 matches; the debut in the third Test of Ian Botham, who took 5 for 21 in the fourth; and Boycott's 100th first-class century. Students of the peculiar might care to note that the Ashes were also recaptured in the year of the Queen's birth (1926) and of her coronation (1953).

Virginia Wade chose this year to win Wimbledon, at her sixteenth attempt, and Liverpool, who won the UEFA Cup in 1976, became the first English club to win the European Cup (Glasgow Celtic were 10 years ahead of them). In the final they beat Borussia Munchengladbach 3-1, and by then had guaranteed their appearance in the competition next time by winning the Football League for the second year in succession.

Liverpool piled the icing on the 1977 cake by beating the European Cup-Winners' Cup holders, SV Hamburg, to take the European Super-Cup. Not so super for Hamburg: after a 1-1 draw at home, they lost 6-0 at Anfield.

ng + Wimbledon glory for Virginia Wade at the sixteenth time of asking + Wimbledon g

VIRGINIA WADE (who at an early stage discarded her first given name of Sarah) was the epitome of what Britain would choose for its leading tennis player: handsome, dramatic, dazzling, elegant and, just to keep you on the edge of your seat, entirely unreliable. Sixteen years she had contested Wimbledon, and on the eve of her 32nd birthday she made it, losing the first set to the unfancied Betty Stove and winning the third 6-1.

She won the US Open in 1968, the Italian in 1971 and the Australian in 1972. Between 1965 and 1985 she played far more rubbers in the Wightman Cup and the Federation Cup than any player in the world.

Hazelwood up in the air +

MIKE HAZELWOOD was outstandingly the greatest tournament water-skier to come from Britain. He was overall men's world champion in 1977, world jump champion in 1979 and 1981, and nine times European overall champion between 1976 and 1986. In 1980 he set a world jump record of 195ft.

+ Boycott is back and more batting records fall + Boyc

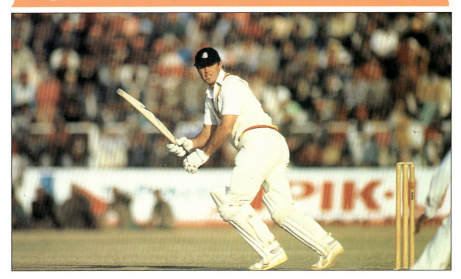

GEOFFREY BOYCOTT was first choice if you had to find a man to bat to save your life. In this summer, after missing 30 Tests, he returned for the third match against Australia to score 107 and 80 not out (batting altogether for more than 12 hours). In the fourth, on his home ground at Headingley, he was last out on 191, having become the first batsman in history to score his 100th century in a Test match (England won by an innings). Even in the fifth, when he scored only 64 runs in two innings, he managed to notch his 5,000th first-class run.

In 1982, 18 years after his debut, he scored his 22nd Test century and became the highest-scoring batsman in international history.

le + Bionic Barry Sheene rides to another world title +

BARRY SHEENE so often had his body put together with metal rods, plates and screws it could hardly be called his own. World 500cc motor cycle champion in 1976 and 1977, he was a bold and brilliant rider with a strong tendency to attract off-track publicity. The worst of his many crashes was at Silverstone in 1982, when he surprisingly emerged alive after being thrown almost 100 yards through the air. Since Sheene in '77, no British rider has won a world title except on a sidecar combination.

CHAMPIONS OF THE WORLD

Bowls
Triples, women - Wales

Canoeing
Slalom K1 - Albert Kerr

Motor Cycling
500cc - Barry Sheene
Formula I - Phil Read
Sidecar - George O'Dell

Powerlifting
82.5kg - Ronald Collins
60kg - Edward Pengelly

Real Tennis
Howard Angus

Rowing
Double sculls - Chris Baillieu and Michael Hart
Eight, lightweight - United Kingdom

Snooker
John Spencer

Speedway
Pairs - Peter Collins and Malcolm Simmons
Team - England

Tug of War
720kg - England

Water-Skiing
Overall - Mike Hazelwood

WORLD RECORDS

Athletics
10 miles - Ian Stewart: 45min 13sec.
150km (world best) - Don Ritchie: 10hr 36min 42sec.
100 miles (w.b.) - Don Ritchie: 11hr 30min 51sec.
4 x 200m relay, women - UK team: 1min 31.6sec.

SPORTS WRITERS' ASSOCIATION
SWA
SPORTSWOMAN OF THE YEAR

1959 Mary Bignal
1960 Anita Lonsbrough
1961 Angela Mortimer
1962 Anita Lonsbrough
1963 Dorothy Hyman
1964 Mary Rand
1965 Marion Coakes
1966 Linda Ludgrove
1967 Beryl Burton
1968 Lillian Board
1969 Ann Jones
1970 Mary Gordon-Watson
1971 HRH The Princess Anne
1972 Mary Peters
1973 Ann Moore
1974 Gillian Gilks
1975 Lucinda Prior-Palmer
1976 Gillian Gilks
1977 Virginia Wade
1978 Sharron Davies
1979 Caroline Bradley
1980 Sharron Davies
1981 Jayne Torvill
1982 Wendy Norman
1983 Jo Durie
1984 Tessa Sanderson
1985 Virginia Holgate
1986 Fatima Whitbread
1987 Fatima Whitbread
1988 Liz McColgan
1989 Yvonne Murray
1990 Tracy Edwards
1991 Liz McColgan

SPORTS TEAM OF THE YEAR

1970 GB women 4 x 800m relay
1971 British Lions rugby
1972 Rodney Pattisson/Chris Davies
1973 England rugby union tour
1974 British Lions rugby
1975 Wightman Cup
1976 Modern pentathlon
1977 Liverpool F.C.
1978 Liverpool F.C.
1979 Nottingham Forest F.C.
1980 Nottingham Forest F.C.
1981 Jayne Torvill/Christopher Dean
1982 Jayne Torvill/Christopher Dean
1983 Jayne Torvill/Christopher Dean
1984 Jayne Torvill/Christopher Dean
1985 Ryder Cup
1986 GB men 4 x 400m relay
1987 Ryder Cup
1988 GB Olympic hockey
1989 GB men's athletics
1990 GB men's athletics
1991 GB men 4 x 400m relay

1978

EIGHTEEN gold medals at the Commonwealth Games in athletics alone was an astonishing performance at a time when Africans were dominating middle and long-distance running. To that add the 1500 metres triumph in the European championships of Steve Ovett, now the world's leader at that distance.

Some astonishment too in tennis, where Britain reached their first Davis Cup final for 41 years (losing to the US 4-1, as they had in 1937) and squeaked home 4-3 in the Wightman Cup at the Albert Hall. Liverpool took the European Cup for the second year running, and Scotland's soccer players were again the only British nation to reach the World Cup finals. As last time, they were eliminated on goal difference, but beat Holland, the eventual finalists.

Captained by Brearley and inspired by Botham, England were unbeaten in the short Test series against Pakistan and New Zealand (won five, drew one). At Wimbledon Navratilova won the first of her five finals with Evert and at St. Andrews Jack Nicklaus won his third Open golf title. One American champion did lose: Ali was beaten on points by Leon Spinks, only his second defeat in 14 years.

+ King of bowls continues his reign + King

DAVID BRYANT this year won his fourth consecutive Commonwealth Games bowls championship, and it would no doubt have been the fifth if there had been bowls in Jamaica in 1966. He was for so long and by so far the best bowler in the world the whole story becomes preposterous: three times world outdoor singles champion, three times world indoor champion, indoor pairs champion (with Tony Allcock) six times in seven years, winner of 16 British and 26 English national titles between 1957 and 1985. And then there is the international Masters tournament at Worthing: nine singles wins in 11 years. The mind continues to boggle.

Teenage prodigies win gold

BRITAIN'S tremendous haul of 33 gold medals from the Commonwealth Games in Edmonton, Canada, bore on them some momentous names. There were the first major track championship wins for David Moorcroft and Scottish sprinter Allan Wells, for instance; the launch into international orbit of the careers of the young Tessa Sanderson and Daley Thompson (who had been competing as a junior the previous year and two years later was to be the Olympic decathlon champion); and the emergence of a 17-year-old boxing prodigy from Northern Ireland named Barry McGuigan.

Capes puts it away

GEOFF CAPES was a policeman who became Britain's favourite shot-putter. Commonwealth Games champion in 1974 and 1978, he competed in three Olympics and was twice the European indoor champion. Weighing around 22 stone, he later achieved great popularity, and success, with his 'strong man' activities on television.

Reardon pockets title again

RAY REARDON, of Wales, is the only man to have won the world snooker championship for four consecutive years (since it became a knock-out tournament in 1969). He first took the title in 1970, held it for four years from 1973 and regained it a second time in 1978. He reached the final for the last time in 1982 and is one of the few world finalists who always looked as though he was enjoying the game.

Teenage Davies wins two Commonwealth gold medals

SHARRON DAVIES was only 13 when she swam for Britain (as a backstroker) in the 1976 Olympics. Two years later she took gold medals in both the 200m and 400m individual medleys at the Edmonton Commonwealth Games. By the 1980 Olympics she was 4½ inches taller and 2½ stones heavier than she had been in Munich and had her finest hour: second to world record breaker Petra Schneider in the 400m medley. Twelve years later Davies had returned to competitive swimming as a glamorous 29-year-old.

CHAMPIONS OF THE WORLD

Darts
Leighton Rees

Equestrianism
Show jumping, team - Great Britain

Gliding
Open - George Lee

Motor Cycling
Formula I - Mike Hailwood

Powerlifting
82.5kg - Ronald Collins
75kg - Peter Fiore
60kg - Edward Pengelly

Rowing
Eight, lightweight - United Kingdom

Shooting
English Match - Alistair Allan
Free rifle, standing - Malcolm Cooper
Small bore, kneeling - John Churchill
Small bore team, kneeling - Great Britain

Snooker
Ray Reardon
Amateur - Cliff Wilson

Speedway
Pairs - Gordon Kennett and Malcolm Simmons

Tug of War
720kg - England
640kg - England

WORLD RECORDS

Athletics
2 miles - Steve Ovett: 8min 13.5sec.
100km (w.b) - Don Ritchie: 6hr 10min 20sec.

Beaten 3-1 by Peru in the World Cup football finals, Scotland left out Graham Souness and saw Willie Johnston fail a dope test after the game.

1979

BRITAIN'S middle-distance runners were now slaughtering the opposition, Seb Coe having joined (and this summer, overtaken) Ovett for what was to prove, with Steve Cram's later help, a decade of international domination during which the record books were frequently rewritten.

Our golfers were girding their loins too. Nick Faldo had won the PGA tournament in 1978 and now Sandy Lyle, only 21, won the European Open and topped the British Order of Merit. The Ryder Cup stayed in America, but a ray of hope shone: European golfers joined the British, and they included the youngest Ryder Cup player ever – 20-year-old Seve Ballesteros, who this year beat Nicklaus and Ben Crenshaw to The Open.

Nottingham Forest succeeded Liverpool as football's European club champions, beating Malmo 1-0 in the final and going on to win the SuperCup with a 2-1 aggregate over Barcelona. In the little world of modern pentathlon, women were now at it. For the past two years a Briton had won their World Cup, and in 1979 it was a young lady called Kathy Tayler, later familiar to viewers of BBC TV travel programmes.

+ Majestic Coe shatters three world records + Maj

SEBASTIAN COE was probably the greatest middle-distance runner of all time. In the space of 42 days this summer he broke three world records – for the 800m, 1500m and the mile (which he ran more than 10sec faster than Bannister had 25 years earlier). In both 1980 and 1984 he won the Olympic 1500m and was second in the 800m, a unique achievement in Olympic history.

He professed to prefer the shorter distance, at which in 1981 he won both the World Cup and the European Cup races and set a new world record. But in the same summer he and Steve Ovett between them broke the mile record three times in 10 days: Coe 3:48.53, Ovett 3:48.40, Coe 3:47.33.

he top + Watt hits the top

GLASGOW boxer Jim Watt won the world lightweight title in April and in just over 18 months had successfully defended it four times, every fight being stopped by the referee. He lost the title, to Alexis Arguello, the first time he defended it outside Glasgow.

+ Keegan scores across Europe as polls are counted + Ke

KEVIN KEEGAN was only the fifth British player in 23 years to be elected European footballer of the year, and is the only one to be honoured twice (on both occasions, 1979 and 1980, he was playing for Hamburg). Among those few, only he and Bobby Charlton have ever also been named player of the year by both the Professional Footballers' Association and the Football Writers' Association. His greatest club achievements in Britain were with Liverpool and Southampton.

+ Double ton for Gower + D

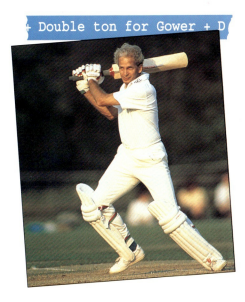

DAVID GOWER may not be regarded as one of the greatest international batsmen, but he was one of the most beautiful to watch. He hooked his first ball in Test cricket for four (against Pakistan in 1978), hit a century off New Zealand that summer and another against Australia in December (the youngest to do so since Compton).

In 1979 he scored 200 not out against India at Edgbaston and he was still only 22. Five years later he first captained England and by 1991 he had scored more than 8000 Test runs at an average of 44.

CHAMPIONS OF THE WORLD

Athletics
Cross-country team - England
Bowls
Indoor - David Bryant
Boxing
Jr.middleweight - Maurice Hope (WBC)
Lightweight - Jim Watt (WBC)
Canoeing
Slalom K1, team - Great Britain
Darts
John Lowe
Motor Cycling
Formula I - Ron Haslam
Motocross, 500cc - Graham Noyce
Powerlifting
82.5kg - Ronald Collins
60kg - Edward Pengelly
Real Tennis
Howard Angus
Rowing
Coxless fours, lightweight - Great Britain
Snooker
Terry Griffiths
Squash
Amateur team - Great Britain
Water Skiing
Jump - Mike Hazelwood

WORLD RECORDS

Athletics
800m - Sebastian Coe: 1min 42.4sec.
1500m - Sebastian Coe: 3min 32.1sec.
1 mile - Sebastian Coe: 3min 49.0sec.
Gliding
750km triangle, women - Karla Karel: 59.2 mph.

THE BRITISH SPORTS TRUST

HELPING THE YOUNG TO HELP THEMSELVES

*Every year in Britain some **fifty million hours** are devoted freely by volunteers to the organisation of sport and active recreation in the community. Without these volunteers, amateur sport in Britain would simply disappear. In recognition of this enormous contribution to the social well-being, as well as to the recreational life, of the nation, the CCPR has created a special Community Sports Leaders Award (CSLA).*

*The **principal aim** of the Award scheme is to help the young, particularly in the disadvantaged areas of the inner cities, by providing trained sports leaders who can guide and inspire youngsters to discover and enjoy the benefits of organised sport and physical recreation. Since the 1982 launching of the CSLA, well over **2,500 courses** have been organised, producing some **35,000 qualified sports leaders**. Such has been the response to the Award Scheme that the CCPR has had to extend its own special staffing provision to cater for the demand for courses from schools, colleges and community organisations.*

*A special body **The British Sports Trust** has been formed, with the object of raising funds for leadership training through the CSLA scheme. The Trust, directed by an advisory Management Committee, brings together, as Vice-Presidents, a number of distinguished figures drawn from commerce, industry, Parliament, show business, the media and sport. Under the Presidency of HRH The Duke of Edinburgh, the Trust has, in a remarkably short time, achieved striking success in improving recreational provision in the community.*

*Of particular note among the many generous contributions, has been the decision of **Hanson plc** to donate £800,000 to the Trust over a period of six years. This has been recognised in the naming of the highest level of the CSLA as "The Hanson Leadership Award".*

TRUSTING TO THE FUTURE

1980

NO OLYMPIC year has ever brought such turmoil. The Soviet Union's military intervention in Afghanistan in 1979 caused international protest, into which some Western governments tried to suck their Olympic teams. President Carter persuaded the United States to boycott the Moscow Games, and Prime Minister Thatcher did her best with the British.

To his eternal credit, British Olympic Association chairman Sir Denis Follows stood firm and let it be known that this was to be a matter of personal choice. The rowing competitors out-voted their officials and went, and the only absentees from the British strength were the equestrian team and the yachtsmen.

Coe and Ovett ran gloriously, each winning the event he was not expected to win; Allan Wells became Britain's first sprint champion since Harold Abrahams (and at 28 the oldest ever); the magnificent Daley Thompson went into the lead from the first decathlon event and was never caught; and it seemed as though Duncan Goodhew would go on beaming for ever.

Back home, in the little town of Southwold, Suffolk, David Bryant was allowed to take £2000 from an indoor bowls tournament win. Professionalism was at last okay.

Moscow Olympic crowd rise to two-lap triumph by Steve Ovett

STEVE OVETT was an international running star from the age of 18 (second in the European championships 1500m) to that of 30, when he won the 5000m at the Edinburgh Commonwealth Games. This year of 1980 was perhaps his best: he took the Olympic 800m in Moscow and broke the world records for the 1500m twice and the mile once.

A year older than Coe, and physically stronger, he ran in three Olympics and won gold medals at the World Cup twice, the European Cup twice and the European championships once. He altogether set six world and 12 national records, and will always be remembered for his devastating speed round the final bend.

Reaching for the sky

TRAMPOLINING lives in the mind of the general public as a recreational activity rather than a competitive sport, but Britain's international success has been considerable. There have been world championships for nearly 50 years, and in 1980 the men's singles was won by Stewart Matthews and the pairs by Matthews and Carl Furrer (who took the singles two years later).

Sue Shotton won the women's title in 1984 and Andrea Holmes, a leading competitor since she was 11 years old, was three times world silver medallist and in 1991 won the European championship and the World Cup.

+ Cousins captures crown +

ONE Olympic gold medal for Britain in solo figure skating was more than most expected to see in a lifetime; for Robin Cousins to repeat John Curry's win was almost unbelievable. They remain the only British men ever to have won any Olympic medal in this discipline. Cousins, a brilliantly athletic skater, had a 2-1 majority from the judges over his German rival, Jan Hoffmann. Some experts thought the Briton unlucky not to get a repeat verdict at the world championships a month later.

+ Forest grow over Europe +

BRITISH football was on the crest of a wave in Europe, winning the Champions' Cup seven times in eight years. After two years of Liverpool triumph, there were now two of Nottingham Forest, for whom John McGovern took the cup after beating Hamburg in the final.

+ Britain's hairless wonder swims to gold in Games +

DUNCAN GOODHEW reached the 1976 Olympic final of the 100m breaststroke while he was still a teenaged student. The next time round, in Moscow, he reached the final of the 200m and gloriously won the gold medal in the 100m. His natural exuberance, his passionate patriotism and the hairlessness he had suffered from childhood subsequently combined appealingly to perpetuate his public personality.

CHAMPIONS OF THE WORLD

Athletics
Cross-country team - England
Badminton
Doubles, women - Nora Perry and Jane Webster
Billiards
Fred Davis
Bowls
David Bryant
Triples - England
Team - England
Indoor - David Bryant
Boxing
Middleweight - Alan Minter
Cycling
Pursuit - Tony Doyle
Darts
Eric Bristow
Equestrianism
Carriage driving, team - Great Britain
Judo
48kg, women - Jane Bridge
Karate
Team - Great Britain
Motor Cycling
Sidecar - Jock Taylor
Powerboating
Formula I - Bob Spalding
Formula III - John Hill
Powerlifting
82.5kg - William West
Rowing
Eight, lightweight - United Kingdom
Shooting
Sporting, women - Anthea Hillyer
Snooker
Amateur - Jimmy White
Speedway
Michael Lee

Pairs - Peter Collins and Dave Jessup
Team - England
Trampolining
Stewart Matthews
Synchro - Stewart Matthews and Carl Furrer
Tug of War
720k - England
640k - England

OLYMPIC CHAMPIONS

Athletics
100m - Allan Wells
800m - Steve Ovett
1500m - Sebastian Coe
Decathlon - Daley Thompson
Ice Skating
Robin Cousins
Swimming
100m breaststroke - Duncan Goodhew

WORLD RECORDS

Athletics
1000m - Sebastian Coe: 2min 13.4sec.
1500m - Steve Ovett: 3min 32.1sec.
1500m - Steve Ovett: 3min 31.4sec.
1 mile - Steve Ovett: 3min 48.8sec.
30 miles (world best) - Jeff Norman: 2hr 42min.
50km (w.b.) - Jeff Norman: 2hr 48min 6sec.
Decathlon - Daley Thompson: 8,622pt.
Decathlon - Daley Thompson: 8,648pt.
Gliding
Triangular distance, women - Karla Karel:
 505.8 miles
Straight distance, women - Karla Karel:
 590.11 miles
Water Skiing
Jump - Mike Hazelwood: 195ft 0in.

1981

ENGLAND'S cricket glories were so dazzling the rest of the year seems in shadow, but there was much to celebrate. Of the well-established champions, Liverpool were back with their third European Cup in five years (1-0 over Real Madrid in the final) and Lester Piggott regained his seat as champion jockey after a break of 10 years.

With his third consecutive win, David Bryant remained the only man to have won the world indoor bowls title. Norma Shaw was getting it right on the greens outside and became the first Briton to win the women's world championship.

There are plenty more significant world firsts to note: a young university student, Richard Fox, won the first of the four titles that were to make him the most respected figure in the history of kayak slalom canoeing. John Prenn took the first of five world rackets singles crowns and Judy Oakes the first of three world powerlifting titles. And there was Torvill and Dean, the ice dancing partnership who in Connecticut skated quietly into the pre-eminent position that was soon to cause the Press of the world to greet them hysterically.

+ Botham and Willis make England dreams come true in Headingley sensation + Botham and

IAN BOTHAM had not gone without success in the four years since his first Test cricket cap, but in this summer series against Australia he performed like a giant. The third Test, at Leeds, was truly the stuff of which dreams are made and it was Botham and Bob Willis who made them come true.

Under Botham's leadership, England had lost the first Test and drawn the second, at the close of which Botham (who had not scored a run in either innings), withdrew from the captaincy. Brearley, who had won the Ashes in Australia in 1979, was reappointed.

Australia scored 401 for 9 declared at Headingley (Botham 6 for 95). England replied with a miserable 174 (Botham 50). In their follow-on, England reached 135 for 7 (still 92 behind) at 3pm on the fourth day. They finished with 356.

Botham hit 100 off his first 87 balls, his second 50 coming in only 40 minutes. His stand of 117 with fast bowler Dilley (56) took only 80 minutes. He was out for 149, but the Australians needed a paltry 130 to win. Time for Willis to enter the dream with the finest spell he ever bowled: 8 for 43 and Australia were all out 18 runs short of the target.

There was more to come. Feeble batting in the fourth Test at Edgbaston (not a 50 in the entire match) left Australia with more than two days to score 151 to take a 2-1 lead in the series. Botham took five wickets for one run in 28 balls, for a final analysis of 5 for 11. Australia totalled 121. The Ashes stayed at home.

Another Davis pots black

Adams the world champion

STEVE DAVIS was to become almost as great a snooker phenomenon as Joe Davis had been. At the age of 23, this year saw him beat Doug Mountjoy 18-12 for the first of his six world titles. In Joe's day it took longer: his last win, in 1946, was 78-67 and two years later brother Fred needed 84 frames to win.

NEIL ADAMS remains the only British male judo player to win a world or Olympic championship, though British women have had outstanding success. On his day, he was the fastest and most exciting judoka in the world. Twelve years later Adams, ever an enthusiast, was still competing in the British Open championships.

CHAMPIONS OF THE WORLD

Angling
Freshwater - Dave Thomas
Billiards
Fred Davis
Bowls
Women - Norma Shaw
Fours, women - England
Team, women - England
Indoor - David Bryant
Canoeing
Slalom K1 - Richard Fox
Slalom K1, team - Great Britain
Slalom C2, team - Great Britain
Darts
Eric Bristow
Gliding
Open - George Lee
Hang Gliding
Team - Great Britain
Ice Skating
Dance - Christopher Dean and Jayne Torvill
Judo
78kg - Neil Adams
Modern Pentathlon
Team, women - Great Britain
Powerboating
Formula III - John Hill
Powerlifting
100kg - Tony Stevens
75kg - Steve Alexander
67.5kg - Edward Pengelly
56kg - Nahrinda Bhairo
75kg, women - Judy Oakes

Rackets
John Prenn
Real Tennis
Chris Ronaldson
Shooting
Sporting - Duncan Lawton
Snooker
Steve Davis
Speedway
Long track - Michael Lee
Water Skiing
Jump - Mike Hazelwood
Slalom - Andy Mapple

WORLD RECORDS

Athletics
800m - Sebastian Coe: 1min 41.73sec.
1000m - Sebastian Coe: 2min 12.18sec.
1 mile - Sebastian Coe: 3min 48.53sec.
1 mile - Steve Ovett: 3min 48.40sec.
1 mile - Sebastian Coe: 3min 47.33sec.
Powerboating
Offshore speed - Ted Toleman: 97.4 mph.
Inshore speed, women - Fiona Brothers: 116.3 mph.
Shooting
Smallbore, prone - Alister Allan: 600 out of 600
Water Skiing
Jump - Mike Hazelwood: 196ft 10in.

1981 IS SPONSORED BY

NATIONAL WESTMINSTER BANK

1981 was the year that Ian Botham inspired England's thrilling Ashes victory over Australia, and Derbyshire edged Northants in a nail-biting conclusion to the first NatWest Trophy final – clearly a fitting year for NatWest's involvement with cricket to begin.

Derbyshire's match was the first in a series of exciting finals. Few cricket lovers will forget John Emburey's match winning boundary for Middlesex in 1984, Derek Randall's heroic but unsuccessful attempt to deny Essex victory in 1985, or Robin Smith's blistering 78 which propelled Hampshire to victory in 1991.

The NatWest Trophy is still going strong today, and promises a lot more exciting cricket moments. But it's only one of many cricket sponsorships enjoyed by NatWest.

National Westminster Bank

NatWest sponsors cricket at every level – from the Trophy down to grass roots level. NatWest promotes the game through the National Cricket Association Awards, NatWest Indoor Cricket Cup, the Cricket Society Coaching scholarships, the NatWest Old England XI, and the NatWest Under 13 Championships for the Ken Barrington Trophy – a regional knockout competition for youngsters who will be the Bothams of the future.

Cricket is an important part of our community programme, a programme which is designed to genuinely "make life easier" – indeed, better – for our customers.

NatWest is delighted to contribute to this celebration of 40 years of sport and hopes that our sponsorship of youth cricket will yield new stars for the next 40 years.

1982

IF WALES had not failed to beat Iceland at home, they would have joined the other three nations of the United Kingdom in football's World Cup finals in Spain. England, boosted by a Bryan Robson goal within 27 seconds of starting their first match, went through with Northern Ireland to the second round, but neither survived. English clubs were still doing well in Europe: this time it was Aston Villa who won the European Cup, beating Bayern Munich 1-0.

In Brisbane, Daley Thompson won the second of his three Commonwealth Games decathlon titles, Steve Cram the first of his two at 1500 metres and Allan Wells the last of his three sprint gold medals. David Moorcroft, holder of the 1500, moved up to 5000m and took that.

Ian Botham was still starring in his hero's role on the cricket field. In the third Test against India at The Oval, England scored 594. Botham hit 208 of them in 226 balls, with four sixes and 19 fours. England's only defeat of the summer was by Pakistan at Lord's, where batting of another kind was on view: Tavare took 350 minutes to score 50, waiting 67 minutes for his first run.

WOMEN from Britain's many fields of sport are seldom less determined, less devoted or less successful than their more highly-publicised male counterparts, and 1982 provides a good example of that. No fewer than eight British women won world championships this year, in seven different sports. Lucinda Green and Jayne Torvill, best-known among them, are highlighted elsewhere, but consider a few of the others.

Karen Briggs, weighing not much more than seven stone, took the first of her four world judo championships, one of which she achieved despite dislocating her shoulder during the final. Mandy Jones fought off the cycling might of Eastern Europe to win the world road race; she also set a world record by covering five kilometres in 3.11 minutes – an average speed of nearly 28mph.

Judy Oakes, better known for winning the Commonwealth Games shot put gold medal this year, also won her

second world powerlifting championship (and did it again six years later). And Wendy Norman, who had already won modern pentathlon's World Cup for women, consolidated her success by becoming the first female world champion of this extremely demanding sport.

> British women supreme: they win eight world championships

Britons the karate kings

BRITAIN'S success in the Japanese martial art of karate is amazing. They first won the world team championship in 1975, and from 1982 took four successive team titles as well as eight individual championships. Three times in four world tournaments British fighters won the heavyweight title, and this year it went to the mighty Jeoff Thompson.

seven different sports + Brit

CHAMPIONS OF THE WORLD

Angling
Freshwater - Kevin Ashurst
Billiards
Rex Williams
Bowls
Indoor - John Watson
Cycling
Road, women - Mandy Jones
Darts
Jocky Wilson
Equestrianism
Three-day event - Lucinda Green
Team - United Kingdom
Ice Skating
Dance - Christopher Dean and Jayne Torvill
Judo
52kg, women - Loretta Doyle
48kg, women - Karen Briggs
Karate
80kg+ - Jeoffrey Thompson
80kg - Patrick McKay
Team - Great Britain
Modern Pentathlon
Women - Wendy Norman
Motor Racing
Kart, 135cc - Michael Wilson
Powerboating
Formula I - Roger Jenkins
Powerlifting
100kg - Tony Stevens
82.5kg, women - Judy Oakes
Rackets
John Prenn
Shooting
Free rifle - Malcolm Cooper
Sporting, women - Anthea Hillyer
Snooker
Alex Higgins
Amateur - Terry Parsons
Trampolining
Carl Furrer
Tug of War
720kg - England

WORLD RECORDS

Archery
Handbow, distance - Alan Webster: 1,231yd 1ft 10in.
Athletics
5000m - David Moorcroft: 13min 00.41sec.
40 miles (world best) - Don Ritchie: 3hr 48min 35sec.
Decathlon - Daley Thompson: 8,704pt.
Decathlon - Daley Thompson: 8,743pt.
4 x 800m relay - Great Britain: 7min 03.89sec.
Cycling
5km, women - Mandy Jones: 6min 41.75sec.
Powerboating
Offshore speed - Ted Toleman: 109.98 mph.
Shooting
English match - Malcolm Cooper: 593/600.

> **Rex Williams twice challenged for the world snooker championship, but his greater success has been at billiards. He first won that world title in 1968 and took it for the seventh time 14 years later**

SPORT FOR THE DISABLED

LESS than 50 years ago, it would have been unthinkable for the severely disabled to take part in any kind of sporting activity, even on a recreational level. Then Professor (later Sir) Ludwig Guttman opened the spinal injuries centre at Stoke Mandeville Hospital and within a year his paraplegic patients were taking part in basketball, archery and table tennis. In 1948, the first Stoke Mandeville Games for the paralysed were held and today disabilities across the world are forgotten as competitors with all kinds of handicaps hurl themselves into unlikely action.

Wheelchair basketball and marathon racing are the best known, but the handicapped have shown that there is almost no end to their sporting potential. The blind play golf, the armless play bowls, the legless ski, the paralysed swim, the cerebally palsied run – none will be denied, and that includes those with a mental handicap.

In 1961, the British Sports Association for the Disabled was founded and that remains the national body responsible for the co-ordination and development of sport and physical recreation for people with a disability. Under their umbrella, there are many specialist organisations.

Probably the biggest among them is the Wheelchair Sports Foundation, which now organises sport for all those confined to a wheelchair, whatever the disability. At the top of the great pyramid is the British Paralympic Association, responsible for the training and selection of those with outstanding sporting ability, who may be chosen to represent the nation at the 'parallel Olympics' which usually follow the able-bodied Games.

The BSAD now organise annual media awards for those who have reported on sport for the disabled, and for many years the Sports Writers' Association have presented an award to the disabled personality of the year.

1983

BRITAIN (with Europe) did not win the Ryder Cup, but it was the closest they had ever come to it on American soil: 14-13. That was not all: Tony Jacklin had taken over as non-playing captain, a job he accepted on condition that the team travelled first class. Not only did he win that concession, but they were booked on Concorde and for the first time were allowed to use their regular caddies for the match. Morale swelled. So did Nick Faldo's wallet: he won £119,416 on the European tour.

They were feeling chuffed in Aberdeen too, where The Dons won both the European Cup and the Super Cup, and around Epsom there was no doubt dancing in the streets when Lester Piggott won his ninth Derby in 32 years of trying. The first world athletics championships were held in Helsinki with only two United Kingdom winners, Steve Cram and the apparently unbeatable Daley Thompson.

England's cricketers were more fallible, losing the Ashes 2-1 in Australia, during which Botham reached 3000 runs and 250 wickets in Test cricket. There was a quirkier record for skipper Willis during the summer, when he became the first man in the world to be not out 50 times in Test cricket.

ld + Torvill and Dean captivate the ice dance world + Torvill

TORVILL and Dean: how the spirit soars at the sound of the phrase! To reduce them to statistics is an insult, but the facts are that they won the world and the European ice dance championships in 1981, 1982 and 1984, the world alone in 1983 (they were injured for the European), and the Olympics in 1984.

As their technical expertise increased, so too did the grace and creative brilliance of their compositions. To the millions who had been rivetted, through television, by the solo figure skating of Curry and Cousins, the partnership of Torvill and Dean added many more millions of fans. It was not unusual to see some at the rinkside reduced to tears by the beauty of their work.

True stars of sport, they remain the only competitors to win the Sports Team of the Year award more than twice. Members of the Sports Writers' Association elected them after each of their four world championships despite some of them doubting whether such a balletic demonstration could be counted among competitive sports.

Their three most memorable free dance creations of 'Mack and Mabel', 'Barnum' and 'Bolero' attracted a plethora of 'perfect and flawless' marks, rising to 14 sixes at their final appearance as amateurs, the world championships in Ottawa. Such finesse in this event will perhaps never again be attained, nor even attempted.

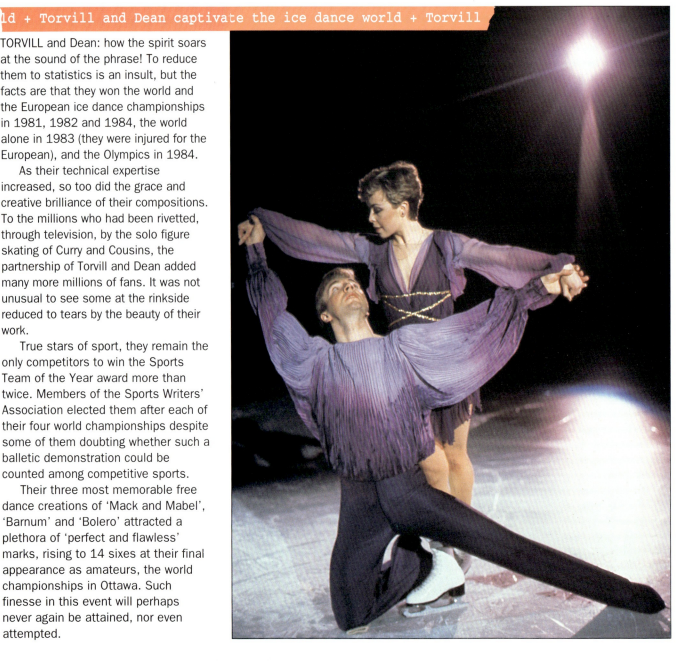

Cram the 1500m king

STEVE CRAM took over from Coe and Ovett as the world's fastest middle-distance runner, but from an early stage was hampered by injury. The 1500m winner at the first world championships in 1983 at the age of 22, he was by then both Commonwealth and European champion, a double he repeated in 1986.

He also won the European Cup 1500m twice, and the 800m as well as the 1500 at the Edinburgh Commonwealth Games of 1986. The previous summer he had broken three world records in 19 days.

Wimbledon win for Lloyd

JOHN LLOYD this year became the first British male tennis player since Fred Perry to get his name on the Wimbledon mixed doubles trophy. He and his Australian partner Wendy Turnbull retained the title in 1984, when Lloyd attained his highest singles world ranking of 23.

CHAMPIONS OF THE WORLD

Athletics
1500m - Steve Cram
Decathlon - Daley Thompson
Road race, women - Wendy Sly

Badminton
Mixed - Nora Perry (with T.Kihlstrom)

Billiards
Rex Williams

Bowls
Indoor - Bob Sutherland

Boxing
Flyweight - Charlie Magri (WBC)

Canoeing
Slalom K1 - Richard Fox
Slalom, team - Great Britain
Slalom K1, women - Elizabeth Sharman

Darts
Keith Deller

Equestrianism
Carriage driving, pairs - Paul Gregory

Ice Skating
Dance - Christopher Dean and Jayne Torvill

Modern Pentathlon
Team, women - Great Britain

Motor Racing
Kart, 250cc - Martin Hines
Kart, 135cc - Michael Wilson

Powerlifting
100kg - Tony Stevens

Rackets
John Prenn

Shooting
Free rifle - Malcolm Cooper
Sporting, women - Anthea Hillyer

Snooker
Steve Davis

Speedway
Pairs - Kenny Carter and Peter Collins

Tenpin Bowling
Doubles - Great Britain

Water Skiing
Racing, women - Liz Hobbs

WORLD RECORDS

Athletics
1500m - Steve Ovett: 3min 30.77sec.
50 miles (world best) - Don Ritchie:
  4hr 51min 49sec.
Decathlon - Daley Thompson: 8.847pt.
50km road, women (w.b.) - Lilian Millian:
  5hr 01min 52sec.

Hang Gliding
Distance - John Pendry: 186.79 miles
Distance, women - Judy Leden: 144.7 miles
Distance, women - Judy Leden: 146.8 miles
Distance (out-and-return), women - Judy Leden:
  50.97 miles

THE INSTITUTE OF PROFESSIONAL SPORT

SET UP under the auspices of the CCPR, the Institute draws together the major professional sports in an organisation dedicated to protecting the welfare of professional sportsmen and women and advancing the image of professional sport.

MEMBERS:

The World Professional Billiards and Snooker Association

The English Bowls Players Association

The Scottish Bowls Players Association

The Professional Cricketers Association

The World Professional Darts Association

The Professional Footballers Association of England and Wales

The Scottish Professional Footballers Association

The Professional Golfers Association

The Jockeys Association of Great Britain

The Rugby League Professional Players Association

The Speedway Riders Association

The Institute's current concerns include:

Monitoring Developments that Impinge on Professional Sport

Training of Professionals for their Post-Sporting Careers

Securing the Welfare of Retired Professionals

Providing Financial Help and Legal Protection

Protecting the Immediate and Long-Term Health of Professionals

Promoting the Positive Image of Professional Sport

The Institute also takes very seriously its responsibility to assist young people who are intent on becoming professionals in gaining a realistic understanding of their career prospects in sport.

1984

TIT-FOR-TAT, the East European nations (with the exception of Romania) boycotted the Los Angeles Olympic Games, the first to have been staged with the avowed intention of making a profit. The Americans had a ball, winning 16 gold medals in track and field alone, but Seb Coe, Daley Thompson and Tessa Sanderson were not to be denied. Nor were the coxed four of the UK rowing team, the first gold medal Britain had won in that sport since 1948.

Torvill and Dean wove their Olympic (and world) magic for the last time and headed for professionalism and marriage (but not to each other). There was not much glitter about England's cricket this year: when they drew with Sri Lanka in August it was their twelfth match without a win. During one defeat in New Zealand England failed, for the first time this century, to total 100 in either innings.

Another humiliating record in the summer, when the West Indies became the first nation ever to win all five Test matches in England. One can hardly speak of it: two were innings defeats and it was in another that the visitors hit 287 in 236 minutes for the second wicket.

Daley the great wins second successive Olympic decathlon title at Los Angeles + Da

DALEY THOMPSON was the greatest all-round track and field athlete of his time, and his time seemed never to stop. He competed in the Montreal Olympics of 1976 (he was still 17 when they opened) and was going for Barcelona four Olympiads and 16 years later. This king of all decathletes was world, Olympic, European and Commonwealth champion from 1982 till his defeat in 1987.

He set four decathlon world records between 1980 and 1984 and won altogether two Olympic gold medals, three Commonwealth and two European; and was aggrieved that national newspapers seemed more interested in Coe, Cram and Ovett.

Sanderson secures the javelin prize she wants most

TESSA SANDERSON'S great javelin rivalry with Fatima Whitbread no doubt spurred them both on to extravagant achievements. There was no more dramatic contest between them than when Sanderson won her second Commonwealth gold medal in 1986, but Tessa (who was also a fine heptathlete) secured the greatest prize when she took the 1984 Olympic title in Los Angeles. She later became a familiar television personality.

Anfield heroes are the champions of Europe once more

LIVERPOOL ascended into an undisputed position as Britain's foremost football club in the mid-Seventies, from which time they won the Football League championship 10 times in 15 years, the European Champion Clubs' Cup four times (this year beating AS Roma in the final) and the F.A. Cup three times (including the 'double' in 1986).

They were served by excellent managers and outstanding players, most of whom would pass the greatest credit for the club's success to the legendary manager Bill Shankly *(left)*.

Man of many parts casts over the world

TONY PAWSON, an all-round sportsman of great ability, re-emerged at an advanced age this year as the world fly-fishing champion, a title won four years later by his son John. Soon after the war Pawson senior hit a century in the Varsity match, opened the batting for Kent and played soccer (as an amateur) for Pegasus, England and Charlton Athletic.

Seve Ballesteros won his second Open, at St. Andrews, after being led for two days by Australian Ian Baker-Finch, playing the Open for the first time.

CHAMPIONS OF THE WORLD

Angling
Fly - Tony Pawson
Billiards
Mark Wildman
Bowls
Fours - England
Team - Scotland
Boxing
Super-middleweight - Murray Sutherland (IBF)
Darts
Eric Bristow
Ice Skating
Dance - Christopher Dean and Jayne Torvill
Judo
48kg, women - Karen Briggs
Karate
80+kg - Jerome Atkinson
80kg - Patrick McKay
70kg - Jim Collins
Team - Great Britain
Motor Cycling
Formula II - Tony Rutter
Powerboating
Formula II - John Hill
Powerlifting
100kg - Tony Stevens
Rackets
Willie Boone
Shooting
Sporting - Gerry Cowler
Sporting, women - Denise Eyre
Snooker
Steve Davis
Amateur, women - Stacey Hillyard
Speedway
Pairs - Peter Collins and Chris Morton
Trampolining
Women - Sue Shotton
Synchro, women - Sue Shotton and Kyrsty McDonald
Team, women - Great Britain
Tug of War
Catchweight - England
560kg - England
Water Skiing
Racing, women - Liz Hobbs

OLYMPIC CHAMPIONS

Athletics
1500m - Sebastian Coe
Decathlon - Daley Thompson
Javelin, women - Tessa Sanderson
Ice Skating
Dance - Christopher Dean and Jayne Torvill
Rowing
Coxed fours - United Kingdom
Shooting
Smallbore, 3-position - Malcolm Cooper

WORLD RECORDS

Athletics
Marathon (world best) - Steve Jones: 2hr 8min 05sec.
Decathlon - Daley Thompson: 8,847pt.
Gliding
750km triangle, women - Pamela Hawkins: 68.96 mph.
Hang Gliding
Out-and-return, women - Judy Leden: 50.97 miles

1985

WHILE British golfers celebrated the greatest year most could remember (the Ryder Cup and The Open championship), cricket fans also threw their caps in the air. England returned from a five-Test tour of India 2-1 up (including their highest score there, 652 for 7, with double centuries for both Gatting and Fowler) and then proceeded to duff up the Australians at home.

This was Gower's greatest summer. He captained the side to a 3-1 Ashes win and scored 166 in the third Test, 215 in the fifth (the highest of his career) and 157 in the sixth. In these last two (both won by an innings) he shared second-wicket partnerships of 331 with Robinson (148) and 351 with Gooch (196). And yet within a year he was to be relieved of the captaincy.

A temporary Briton, Zola Budd, won the world cross-country championship and a 17-year-old unseeded German named Boris Becker devastated Wimbledon. There was real devastation in football: 39 fans died at the Heysel Stadium in Brussels (Liverpool v Juventus) and 56 at a fire in the Bradford grandstand.

Late charge from Lyle to win The Open + Late cha

SANDY LYLE was the first British winner of The Open golf championship since Tony Jacklin in 1969. After three rounds at Sandwich, he was two behind the joint leaders, Bernard Langer and David Graham. In difficult conditions, they both shot 75 on the final round, while Lyle had a magnificent 70 for an aggregate 282 (two over par). In 1988 he became the first Briton to win the US Masters.

In the Ryder Cup at The Belfry, the United States took the opening foursomes 3-1, but were only one point ahead at the end of the first day and two behind after the second. The Europeans enjoyed a final day of unlikely glory and took the Cup 16-11.

+ Britons still hang high

HANG GLIDING is another of those overlooked sports at which Britain excels, despite being short of suitable vantage points from which to launch major flights. In the six world championships between 1981 and 1991, they won the team title four times. John Pendry became the solo world champion in 1985 and Judy Leden took the women's crown in 1987 and 1991 as well as setting a number of impressive records.

+ Slalom canoeists on the crest of another wave + Slal

RICHARD FOX this year won the third of his four world canoe slalom championships, making him without doubt the most brilliant operator of a kayak the sport had ever seen. Of the five championships held between 1981 and 1989, he missed out in only 1987, when Elizabeth Sharman took the women's K1 title. Britain won the men's K1 team prize in every one of those years except 1989.

Slalom canoeing was contested on an artificial course at the Munich Olympics of 1972. It was not included again until the Barcelona Games 20 years later, on a river high in the Pyrenees.

Taylor pots final black +

DENNIS TAYLOR won the most memorable of all world snooker finals. He potted the final black in the final frame of his match with Steve Davis, who had just missed it. Davis had hurtled into an early lead, leaving Taylor (in the words of one reporter) 'looking like a sick owl resigned to being savaged by an eagle'.

CHAMPIONS OF THE WORLD

Angling
Freshwater - David Roper
Freshwater team - Great Britain

Athletics
Cross-country, women - Zola Budd

Billiards
Ray Edmonds

Bowls
Fours, women - Scotland
Indoor - Terry Sullivan

Boxing
Jr.lightweight - Barry Michael (IBF)
Featherweight - Barry McGuigan (WBA)

Canoeing
Slalom K1 - Richard Fox

Darts
Eric Bristow,

Gliding
15m class - Brian Spreckley

Hang Gliding
John Pendry
Team - Great Britain

Motor Cycling
Formula II - Brian Reid
Motocross, 500cc - David Thorpe

Motor Racing
Sports car - Derek Bell
Kart, 135cc - Michael Wilson

Powerboating
Formula I - Bob Spalding
Formula II - John Hill

Powerlifting
100kg - Tony Stevens
90kg - David Caldwell
67.5kg - Edward Pengelly

Rackets
Willie Boone

Real Tennis
Chris Ronaldson

Rowing
Double sculls, lightweight, women - Lin Clark and Beryl Crockford

Shooting
Sporting - Barry Simpson
5-trap universal trench - Chris Cloke

Snooker
Dennis Taylor
Amateur, women - Alison Fisher

Speedway
Long track - Simon Wigg

Squash
Team, women - England

WORLD RECORDS

Athletics
1500m - Steve Cram: 3min 29.67sec.
1 mile - Steve Cram: 3min 46.32sec.
2000m - Steve Cram: 4min 51.39sec.
30km (world best) - Steve Jones: 1hr 28min 40sec.
20 miles (w.b.) - Steve Jones: 1hr 35min 22sec.

1985 IS SPONSORED BY
BRITISH AIRWAYS

1985 could have been better for England cricket captain Mike Gatting. He flew on British Airways to challenge the West Indies XI – and returned with a broken nose and two black eyes.

Boxer Barry McGuigan had better luck – when 9,000 supporters flew from Belfast to London to watch him win the world title.

Scores of other sporting personalities sampled the services of the world's largest international airline – voted Airline of the Year in a national poll.

1985 saw British Airways expand its already unrivalled route network, restyle staff uniforms, unveil Concorde's new livery and move longhaul services to Heathrow's new Terminal 4 – all part of its commitment to putting customers first.

Small wonder so many sports people fly British Airways to face their opponents and, maybe, scoop that precious title.

The airline invests years of research and millions of pounds on meeting customers' needs, including sporting customers.

BRITISH AIRWAYS
The world's favourite airline.

Alone among world airlines, it maintains a Sports Bureau to service travel arrangements for this multi-million pound industry. Peter Barry and five staff advise on flights and prices, make thousands of bookings and ensure fencers and footballers alike arrive ready to face their rivals. Customers range from local soccer teams to carrying the entire UK Olympic team to Barcelona.

Its staff include at least one eminent sports personality – cricketer Jan Brittan, who helped put women's cricket on the sporting map.

1985 sponsorships included yachtsman Robin Knox-Johnstone in his catamaran **British Airways I,** *the British Hunter horse trials and even the World Elephant Polo championships!*

British Airways is delighted to take part in this book. We look forward to playing an equally full part in sport's next 40 years.

1986

EDINBURGH staged its second Commonwealth Games in some financial discomfort. England's runners had a whale of a time regardless, their men winning all the gold medals from 400 metres to 10,000. Steve Cram did the 800/1500 double, as did Kirsty Wade for Wales; and the first women's 10,000m went to Liz Lynch (later McColgan). In the European championships, British runners had their finest haul of six gold medals. Almost inevitably, Daley Thompson won the decathlon in both championships. Tessa Sanderson took the Commonwealth javelin with 69.80m, but Fatima Whitbread triumphed in the European with a world record of 77.44m.

England, Scotland and Northern Ireland all qualified for the football World Cup finals in Mexico. Only England made progress in a tournament in which the average number of goals scored per match was 2.21, the lowest in history. In Switzerland 32 years earlier the average was 5.38.

The cricketing year began with England returning from the West Indies without a Test win and without a Test century. Highest score was Gower's 90, and his was the highest average, 37. In the closing days of the year, however, England retained the Ashes by beating Australia by an innings and 14 runs in Melbourne.

GARY LINEKER, the most popular central striker England had found since Nat Lofthouse, was top scorer of the World Cup competition in Mexico. His six goals included a hat-trick against Poland, the only goals England scored in their three games of the first pool. England lost in the notorious quarter-final against Argentina – one goal from Maradona's foot and one from his hand beating one from Lineker's head. The Spurs star scored four goals in the next World Cup too (Italy 1990) and by the start of the 1991-92 season had netted 45 goals from 68 matches. He was then made England's captain.

+ Lineker keeps ahead of the world in Mexico +

+ Grand six for Mansell +

NIGEL MANSELL won six Grands Prix in 1986 to finish second in the motor racing drivers' championship, only two points behind Alain Prost. The British driver was runner-up again in 1987 and 1991, and opened the next season with a record five straight wins.

Gatting strikes gold in his rush on Australia

MIKE GATTING began his tenure of the England captaincy inauspiciously, taking over from Gower in a series lost 2-1 to India and going on to lose 1-0 to New Zealand. A pugnacious cricketer first capped in 1977, he took England to Australia in 1986 and won the Ashes, the one-day World Series and an O.B.E.

Alas, pitfalls were ahead: first the embarrassing confrontation with umpire Shakoor Rana on the Pakistan tour and then an indiscretion at home that caused him to be dropped from the captaincy during the 1988 Tests. The following year Gatting agreed to lead an unofficial tour of South Africa.

Rowing sensation by Redgrave

STEVEN REDGRAVE is the only oarsman to have achieved something like star status in Britain. He already held one Olympic gold when this year, at the Commonwealth Games, he pulled off a sensational hat-trick: gold medals at single sculls, coxless pairs and coxed fours. In the next two years he won world and Olympic gold with Andrew Holmes, *(right)* and in 1991 regained that coxless pairs title with Matthew Pinsent.

CHAMPIONS OF THE WORLD

Athletics
Cross-country, women - Zola Budd
Cross-country team, women - England

Bowls
Indoor - Tony Allcock
Indoor pairs - David Bryant and Tony Allcock

Boxing
Light-heavyweight - Dennis Andries (WBC)
Welterweight - Lloyd Honeyghan

Cycling
Pursuit - Tony Doyle

Darts
Eric Bristow

Equestrianism
Three-day event - Virginia Leng
Three-day event, team - United Kingdom

Judo
61kg, women - Diane Bell
56kg, women - Ann Hughes
48kg, women - Karen Briggs

Karate
80+kg - Vic Charles
Team - Great Britain

Motor Racing
Sports car - Derek Bell

Powerboating
Formula II - Jonathan Jones (equal)

Powerlifting
100kg - Tony Stevens
60kg, women - Rita Bass

Rackets
John Prenn

Rowing
Coxed pairs - Great Britain
Double sculls, lightweight -
 Carl Smith and Alan Whitwell

Shooting
English match rifle - Malcolm Cooper
Free rifle, 3 x 20 - Malcolm Cooper
Free rifle, 3 x 40 - Malcolm Cooper
Sporting, universal trench - Kevin Gill
Sporting, women, - Anthea Hillyer

Snooker
Joe Johnson

Tug of War
640kg - England

WORLD RECORDS

Athletics
30 miles, women - Ann Franklin:
 3hr 28min 12sec.
50km, women - Ann Franklin: 3hr 36min 58sec.
40 miles, women - Ann Franklin:
 4hr 47min 27sec.
Javelin, women - Fatima Whitbread: 77.44m.

Gliding
Triangular distance - Robbie Robertson:
 851.68 miles

THE INSTITUTE OF SPORTS SPONSORSHIP

Sponsorship of sport in the United Kingdom has increased more than ten-fold in the last fifteen years, from £22 million in 1975 to an estimated £250 million. It therefore represents a major source of funding for sport at all levels and, in view of its growing importance, the decision was taken in 1985 to establish the Institute of Sports Sponsorship (ISS) as the representative body for business sponsorship of sport, under the Presidency of HRH The Duke of Edinburgh. The members of the ISS make a significant contribution to sport across a wide spectrum of sporting activities, from major televised sports to "grass roots" events.

In pursuit of its aim to improve both the quality and quantity of sports sponsorship, the ISS has been active in establishing and maintaining contacts with government, MPs, the media and national and international sports organisations. An example of recent activity has been the ISS's submission to the government's Review of Sport and Active Recreation, which resulted in the ISS

being given responsibility for running a new £ for £ sponsorship scheme, with £3 million being made available for "grass roots" sports in England alone over 1992/93. In addition, the ISS "Business of Sport" Exhibition was held in Strasbourg, attended by Euro MPs and European Commission, which led to the foundation of an Inter-Group for Sport, chaired by Euro MP, John Tomlinson. On the media front, the ISS has been active in protecting sponsors' interests during the preparation of the ITC Code of Programme Sponsorship, ensuring significant changes were made to the benefit of the sponsors of televised events and intervening to help protect the rights of event sponsors.

1987

GOLF seized us by the throat and pinned millions to their armchairs this year. Even those who had never swung a club were captivated when Nick Faldo stole The Open on the last day, the first Briton to win the silver claret jug since Tony Jacklin in 1970. Then, glory be, the Europeans inflicted the first Ryder Cup defeat on the Americans on their own soil. Two more historic golf wins later: Ian Woosnam became the first Briton to win the world matchplay title (Lyle was second) and Laura Davies the first to win the women's US Open.

Less to smile about elsewhere: only one gold medal from the world athletic championships in Rome and though England's cricketers (under Mike Gatting) started the year by winning the World Series in Australia, they then lost two Test series to Pakistan (who hit 708 at The Oval, 217 of them off Botham).

There was a warm glow from hockey. England's men and women both reached the finals of their European championships, where each lost to Holland in penalty shoot-outs after extra time. Better still, England staged the World Cup at Willesden and reached that final, losing 2-1 to Australia.

les + Faldo wins The Open on the 18th as Azinger's nerve crumbles + Faldo wins The O

NICK FALDO suffered less from the rain that fell over Muirfield's Open golf than most of his American rivals. He followed his first round 68 with a 69 that put him in second place and held that after his third round of 71. One stroke down on Paul Azinger, Faldo gripped his chance and never let go.

He played a beautiful five-iron to the 18th green, over-putted by four feet and sunk the second putt for another 71. Behind him, Azinger's nerve crumbled. He took six at the 17th, hooked his five-iron into the back slope of an 18th bunker and left himself a 30ft putt to force a play-off. That was too much: glory (and £75,000) to Faldo.

Though he did not follow this, as Jacklin did, by winning the US Open, even greater achievements were in store for Faldo. Three years later he became the first British golfer since Henry Cotton to win The Open twice and the only golfer other than Jack Nicklaus to win the US Masters twice in succession.

Mixed cup back in Britain after 51 years + Mixed cup ba

WIMBLEDON had grown accustomed to the absence of Britons in the second week and gave a tremendous welcome on the last day to Jeremy Bates and Jo Durie, the first British pair for 13 years to contest any doubles final. When they took the £27,900 prize, they became the first British mixed doubles champions since Fred Perry and Dorothy Round in 1936.

Ginny Leng champion again

VIRGINIA LENG succeeded Lucinda Green as Britain's supreme exponent of three-day event riding. Already world and European champion (on Priceless), she this year retained the European title on Night Cap (riding clear in both the cross-country and the show jumping) and was to do it again in 1989 on Master Craftsman.

That made an unprecedented three successive European championships. Mrs Leng (nee Holgate) also won the British trials classics of Badminton (twice) and Burghley (a record five times, of which two were European championships).

+ Javelin hits world target +

FATIMA WHITBREAD, already the javelin world record holder and European champion, became the world champion in Rome. Despite continuing problems with her throwing shoulder, she held off the challenge of Petra Felke to take the title with 76.64m – a distance that in 1952 would have won her the Olympic gold medal for men.

Dogged by injury and illness, she took the Olympic silver medal in 1988, but had to retire in 1992.

CHAMPIONS OF THE WORLD

Angling
Fly - Brian Leadbetter
Fly team - England
Freshwater - Clive Branson
Freshwater team - England

Athletics
Javelin, women - Fatima Whitbread

Billiards
Norman Dagley

Bowls
Indoor - Tony Allcock
Indoor pairs - Tony Allcock and David Bryant

Boxing
Welterweight - Lloyd Honeyghan (WBC/IBF)
Jr.welterweight - Terry Marsh (IBF)

Canoeing
Slalom K1, team - Great Britain
Slalom K1, women - Elizabeth Sharman
Canoe sailing - Robin Wood

Darts
John Lowe

Golf
Matchplay - Ian Woosnam
World Cup - Wales

Hang Gliding
Women - Judy Leden
Team, women - United Kingdom

Judo
61kg, women - Diane Bell
52kg, women - Sharon Rendle

Motor Cycling
Sidecar - Steve Webster

Powerboating
Offshore, Class I - Steve Curtis

Powerlifting
125kg - John Neighbour
99kg, women - Jacqueline Pepper

Rackets
John Prenn

Real Tennis
Doubles, women - Katrina Allen and Lesley Ronaldson

Rowing
Coxless pairs - Andrew Holmes and Steven Redgrave

Shooting
Sporting - A J Smith

Snooker
Steve Davis
Amateur - Darren Morgan

Squash
Team, women - England

1987 IS SPONSORED BY
COURAGE

COURAGE celebrated its bi-centenary in 1987 and it is, therefore, appropriate that the company should seek to salute Britain's sporting achievements of that year.

From its origins on the South Bank of the Thames to its current international success, Courage has represented all that is best in British brewing heritage. Quality products and customer service have always been hallmarks of the Courage tradition and remain so today.

As the product range has widened, so too have the exciting promotional activities employed. High profile advertising and marketing have been to the fore, and so too has sponsorship of the best of British sporting endeavour.

COURAGE
— EST 1787 —

The Courage programme of sports sponsorship has embraced a very wide range of sporting activity. In rugby union, rugby league, soccer, cricket, golf, athletics, snooker, horse racing, squash, tennis, polo and in many other sports, the company's support has been valued. From grass roots events to the Courage Clubs Championship and the Foster's Oval, the accent has been on partnership with sport to produce enjoyment and success.

In the local and national community Courage will continue to play its part in the promotion of all that is best in British sport.

1988

WITH the first boycott-free Olympic Games since 1972, medals were never going to be easy to win, and though our track-and-field athletes came home with eight, none of them were gold. Britain's outstanding successes in Seoul came from Adrian Moorhouse in the pool and from the less populated areas of hockey, shooting, sailing and rowing, where Steven Redgrave took his second Olympic gold medal.

On the golf courses all was still going remarkably well. Sandy Lyle won the US Masters, the British Masters and the world matchplay, in which he beat Faldo, who failed in the play-off with Curtis Strange to add this year's US Open title to last year's British Open. At Sandwich, Britain's women retained the Curtis Cup for the first time in its 56-year history.

There was cricket too, but that is another story: a dismal series against West Indies in which England comprehensively lost four matches, drew one and got through four captains – Gatting, Emburey, Chris Cowdrey and Gooch. Hopes that the footballers would restore face were short-lived: only England qualified for the European Championship finals, where they lost to the Republic of Ireland, Holland and the USSR.

+ Second gold for Cooper, the marksman nobody in the world can match + Second

MALCOLM COOPER this year won his second consecutive Olympic gold medal for small-bore rifle shooting (three-position). One point behind team-mate Alister Allan after 120 rounds, Cooper won with 99.3 in the final shoot-out.

There has never been a British marksman to equal him. Any attempt to list his other international triumphs is bound to be incomplete, but try this for a start: six world championships, 12 world records, 11 European championships and four Commonwealth Games gold medals (including one pairs win with his wife, Sarah). In Olympic, world, European and Commonwealth contests alone he won 46 medals between 1977 (when he was 30) and 1988.

Knock-out king Honeyghan regains the welterweight crown

LLOYD HONEYGHAN was a charismatic welterweight who took the world title from Don Curry in 1986 and defended it with startling success three times within a year, two of the fights between them lasting only three rounds. He was beaten by Jorge Vaca in 1987 but regained the crown from him in March of this year with a third-round knock-out. He lost his WBC title to Marlon Starling in 1989 and unsuccessfully challenged Mark Breland for the WBA version in 1990.

Moorhouse by a whisker + Mo

ADRIAN MOORHOUSE was only 17 when he won his first Commonwealth Games gold medal. He went to the Seoul Olympics as reigning European champion at 100m breaststroke and took the gold medal by one-hundredth of a second. The next year he set a new world record at that distance of 1min 01.49sec, a time he has since twice matched. He won the European Open Cup in 1990 and was second in the 1991 world championships.

Hockey reaches the top

BRITISH hockey had been gradually creeping up the ratings both of international success and of popularity. That stemmed not just from the bronze medal at the 1984 Olympics, but from the outstanding achievements of the Southgate club in the late 1970s, when they were European champions for three successive years.

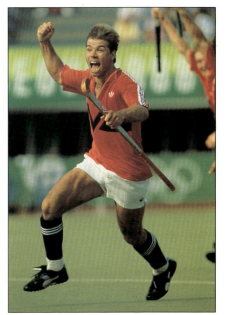

Runners-up in both the World Cup of 1986 and the European Cup of 1987, Britain were well in the frame for Seoul. Nevertheless, their win in the Olympic final against West Germany produced euphoria such as had not been seen since the modern pentathletes won in Montreal.

CHAMPIONS OF THE WORLD

Angling
Fly - John Pawson
Freshwater team - England

Bowls
David Bryant
Team - England
Women - Janet Acland
Team, women - England
Indoor - Hugh Duff

Boxing
Welterweight - Lloyd Honeyghan (WBC)
Flyweight - Duke McKenzie (IBF)

Canoeing
Marathon C2 - Andrew and Steve Train

Cycling
Points, women - Sally Hodge

Darts
Bob Anderson

Golf
Matchplay - Sandy Lyle
Amateur team - Great Britain and Ireland

Karate
65kg - Tim Stephens
60kg - Abdu Shaher
Team - Great Britain

Motor Cycling
Sidecar - Steve Webster

Motor Racing
Sports car - Martin Brundle
Kart, 135cc - Michael Wilson

Powerboating
Offshore, Class II - Roger Fletcher

Powerlifting
90+kg, women - Myrtle Augle
82.5kg, women - Judy Oakes

Rackets
James Male

Shooting
Sporting - John Bidwell

Squash
Team, women - England

Tug of War
640kg - England
560kg - England

Water Skiing
Racing - Stephen Moore

OLYMPIC CHAMPIONS

Hockey
Men - United Kingdom

Rowing
Coxless pairs - Andrew Holmes and Steven Redgrave

Sailing
Star class - Michael McIntyre and Philip Vaile

Shooting
Smallbore, 3-position - Malcolm Cooper

Swimming
100m breaststroke - Adrian Moorhouse

WORLD RECORDS

Athletics
200 miles, women (world best) - Hilary Walker: 39hr 9min 3sec.
48 hours, women (w.b.) - Hilary Walker: 227 miles 757 yards.

Britain's record in ultra-marathon running is amazing. At anything from 50 miles to a week, both men and women frequently prove unbeatable.

1989

ATHLETICS leaped up the excitement graph when Britain won the European Cup, 12 points clear of East Germany. They had nine wins there (including both relays) and another three in the World Cup, as well as a gold medal for John Regis in the world indoor championships. Not that golf was losing much ground: the Ryder Cup stayed in Britain after a pulsating draw at The Belfry; Faldo won the US Masters with a 30-foot birdie putt and took the world matchplay title; and Ian Woosnam was only one stroke off the US Open.

Endeavouring to get their house back in order, the cricket authorities recalled as skipper David Gower, one of the few who had not captained England in 1988. It didn't do the trick. In the six summer Tests, the Australians never failed to top 400 in their first innings and twice were over 600.

The fifth Test was notably galling, despite a thrilling century from Robin Smith in 150 balls. The Aussie openers batted through the first day, eventually compiling a record stand of 329. They declared at 602 for 6 and England lost by an innings and 180 runs.

+ Britain's fastest sprinter proves too fast for the rest of the world + Britain's fa

LINFORD CHRISTIE, often captain of the athletics team, is the finest sprinter Britain has produced for at least 60 years. He stormed into world reckoning in 1986, winning the European indoor and outdoor 100m. Second to Carl Lewis in the 1988 Olympics (after Ben Johnson's removal), he hit his peak this summer (at the age of 29) and won the 100m in both the European Cup and the World Cup finals.

At the European championships of 1990 he took gold in the 100m and bronze in the 200m, and in 1991 won the European Cup sprint again.

Milton the grey star + Mi

JOHN WHITAKER and his beautiful grey horse Milton are the stars of the show jumping circuit even when they don't win. That is not often. In 1989 they won the European championship, in 1990 the World Cup and the silver medal in the world championships. The partnership retained the World Cup in 1991, during which they won more than £180,000 in prize money for the horse's owners.

World beater Andries keeps punching his way back to the top

DENNIS ANDRIES was at least 32 before he first won the WBC version of the world light-heavyweight boxing title in 1986, beating J. R. Williamson, and thereafter showed extraordinary determination and stamina. He lost it to Thomas Hearns in 1987, got it back by beating Tony Willis two years later and was stopped by Jeff Harding four months after that.

In 1990 (then 37 at a conservative estimate) Andries won the return bout. He beat off two challenges before succumbing to Harding once more in 1991.

Champion out-rides them all

PETER SCUDAMORE won 221 races in the 1988-89 National Hunt season, 72 more than any jockey before him. Many were for the trainer Martin Pipe, whose stable owners were enriched by £589,460. Seven times champion jump jockey, Scudamore's figure dropped to 170 in the following season, but Pipe's went up to £792,544.

During the 1990-91 season Scudamore broke his leg and was out for 10 weeks. He was still the champion, with 141 wins from 423 rides, and trainer Pipe pulled in more than £1 million. The owner with the most winners was Pipe Scudamore Racing plc.

CHAMPIONS OF THE WORLD

Angling
Freshwater - Thomas Pickering
Billiards
Mike Russell
Bowls
Indoor - Richard Corsie
Indoor pairs - Tony Allcock and David Bryant
Boxing
Light-heavyweight - Dennis Andries (WBC)
Cruiserweight - Glenn McCrory (IBF)
Flyweight - Dave McCauley (IBF)
Canoeing
Slalom K1 - Richard Fox
Cycling
Pursuit - Colin Sturgess
Darts
Jocky Wilson
Golf
Matchplay - Nick Faldo
Hang Gliding
Robbie Whittall
Team - Great Britain
Judo
52kg, women - Sharon Rendle
48kg, women - Karen Briggs
Motor Cycling
Formula I - Carl Fogarty
Sidecar - Steve Webster
Motor Racing
Kart, 250cc - Tim Parrott
Kart, 135cc - Michael Wilson
Powerboating
Formula II - Jonathan Jones
Powerlifting
110kg - John Neighbour

Real Tennis
Women - Penny Fellows
Doubles, women - Alex Garside and Sally Grant
Shooting
Sporting - A J Smith
Snooker
Steve Davis
Speedway
Team - England
Long track - Simon Wigg
Squash
Women - Martine Le Moignan
Team, women - England
Surfing
Martin Potter
Wall Climbing
World Cup - Simon Nadin

WORLD RECORDS

Athletics
10km road, women - Liz McColgan:
  30min 38sec.
200km, women (world best) - Eleanor Adams:
  19hr 28min 48sec.
24 hours, women (w.b.) - Eleanor Adams:
  240.169km.
500km, women (w.b.) - Eleanor Adams:
  77hr 53min 46sec.
500 miles, women (w.b.) - Eleanor Adams:
  134hr 1min 59sec.
Swimming
100m breaststroke - Adrian Moorhouse:
  1min 01.49sec.
200m breaststroke - Nick Gillingham:
  2min 12.90sec.

1990

WORDS can hardly recapture the excitements of this summer. From Italy the World Cup, probably seen by more people around the globe than had ever watched a sports meeting before; from fairways and greens in America and Britain, the joy of seeing Nick Faldo established as the best golfer in the world; from Split, eight athletic gold medals for Britain in the European championships; and from cricket grounds all over England, more runs scored than had ever been seen before.

Even Graham Gooch's 333 against India was not the highest score of the summer: Fairbrother hit 366 for Lancashire (863 all out) against Surrey (707). Somerset's Cook scored 313 not out against Glamorgan, there were 32 double centuries, 428 tons and 15 innings totals of more than 500.

There were severe disappointments about the World Cup. The average number of goals per game was the lowest ever (2.21) and England did not score enough of them. They beat Cameroon 3-2 after extra time in the quarter-finals, but scored only six goals in their other seven matches. Most critically, they missed two penalties in the semi-final shoot-out with West Germany after the drawn game.

+ Gooch in his greatest year: triple ton takes him past Bradman record + Gooch in h

GRAHAM GOOCH had the year of his life. In the first Test of his first tour as captain, England beat the West Indies for the first time in 16 years. At home he led England to short series wins against New Zealand and India, and in the first innings of the first Indian Test he hit the first triple century for England since 1965 and the sixth highest score in Test history.

He scored another 123 in the second innings, giving him the greatest number of runs ever scored by one man in a Test match; and 116 in the first innings of the next match. He averaged 125 for that series and amassed a total for the summer's six Tests of 1,058 runs, beating Bradman's 60-year-old record of 974.

With another eight centuries in county cricket, the Essex and England skipper finished with 2,746 runs at an average of 101. He went on the next year to lead England to their first win at home over the West Indies since 1969.

Faldo better than ever +

NICK FALDO exceeded even his 1987 brilliance when this year he won the US Masters (on the second extra hole of the play-off with Ray Floyd), missed the US Open play-off by a whisker on the last green, and won his second British Open by five strokes from Mark McNulty and Payne Stewart. Faldo was only the second man to retain the Masters and the second Briton to win The Open twice.

Backley the best of all

STEVE BACKLEY is the first British male javelin thrower to be ranked number one in the world. After a tremendous season in 1989 – he won the World Cup, the European Cup, the Grand Prix final and the World Student Games, all at the age of 20 – he did even better in 1990. Backley twice broke the world record and won the European championships.

Gascoigne dazzles the world

PAUL GASCOIGNE hysteria reached a disturbing level after the World Cup, during which he received a yellow card and shed the famous tears and after which he was voted BBC TV Sports Personality of the Year. The tremendous talent he exercised throughout the tournament led to his becoming the most valuable (and the most marketable) footballer in Britain, positions put in doubt by a serious injury at the start of the 1991 F.A. Cup Final. The Tottenham player appeared to bring the disaster on himself, and might have been sent off had he not been carried off. The damage and its treatment caused the delay of Gascoigne's transfer to Lazio, of Italy.

CHAMPIONS OF THE WORLD

Angling
Freshwater - Robert Nudd

Archery
Field, women - Susan Davies
Field (compound), women - Ann Shepherd

Billiards
Mike Russell

Bowls
Indoor - John Price
Indoor pairs - Tony Allcock and David Bryant
Indoor, women - Fleur Bougard

Boxing
Light-heavyweight - Dennis Andries (WBC)

Croquet
Robert Fulford

Darts
Phil Taylor

Flying
Microlight - Richard Meredith-Hardy
Microlight, team - Great Britain

Golf
Matchplay - Ian Woosnam

Karate
Team - Great Britain

Motor Racing
Kart, 250cc - Tim Parrott
Rally, women - Louise Aitken-Walker

Powerlifting
56kg - Gary Simes

Rackets
Doubles - James Male and John Prenn

Shooting
Free rifle, 3 x 40 - Malcolm Cooper
Free rifle, kneeling - Malcolm Cooper
Sporting - Mick Rouse
Sporting, women - Anthea Hillyer

Snooker
Stephen Hendry

Speedway
Long track - Simon Wigg

Squash
Team, women - England

WORLD RECORDS

Athletics
Javelin - Steve Backley: 89.58m.
Javelin - Steve Backley: 90.98m.
1500m, indoors - Peter Elliott: 3min 34.21sec.
200km, women (world best) - Eleanor Adams: 19hr 0min 31sec.

1990 IS SPONSORED BY
FOOTBALL TRUST

NINETEEN-ninety was a key year in the life of the Football Trust. The Government selected the Trust as the vehicle for channelling grant aid to clubs for the implementation of the Taylor report. The Chancellor's 1990 Budget reduced pool betting duty which provided for some £20m a year to be released to the Trust. The Trust continues also to be funded from the Spotting-the-Ball competition run by Littlewoods, Vernons and Zetters, providing some £12m a year.

The Trust is helping the game at all levels, in raising standards of safety and comfort. Grants are made for new stadia, seating, new stands, roofing, community schemes, facilities for people with disabilities, policing and stewarding and closed circuit television equipment.

Non-League clubs are not forgotten. Essential safety work, pitch and dressing room improvements and community schemes all receive generous grant aid. The Trust also supports the development of football facilities at schools and colleges, charitable and voluntary organisations, and youth and community groups. Lord Aberdare, the Trust's Chairman, has his own discretionary fund to help the grassroots of the game particularly with the provision of kit and equipment.

Helping the game

1991

HAVING won none of the winter Tests in Australia, it was a rare pleasure for England to take the first of the summer Tests – the first home win against the West Indies since 1969. The last Test was even better. By then the visitors were 2-1 up, but England passed 400 against them for the first time in 33 matches and got them out for 176 (the amazing Tufnell, 6 for 25 in 15 overs). That was enough for a win and a squared series, even though Tufnell's second-innings analysis was one for 150.

Best news about football was that England's clubs were allowed back in European competition again, and celebrated by Manchester United taking the Cup-Winners' Cup with a 2-1 victory over Barcelona. The trip gave the promise of considerable lightening of the traditional hooligan clouds, a sign as welcome as the win itself.

And the athletes, bless them, were still at it. The men beat both Germany and the USSR in head-to-head matches, won eight gold medals at the European Cup final as well as the 4 x 400 metres relay, and won the marathon World Cup – contested at the eleventh anniversary of the London marathon.

McColgan leaves the rest of the world in her wake

LIZ McCOLGAN won Britain's only individual gold medal at the world athletics championships this year. Though it was far from her best 10,000m time, she was nearly 21sec ahead of the next woman to finish. Mrs McColgan (nee Lynch) has built up a long-distance running record that places her among the all-time greats.

She won the Commonwealth Games 10,000m in 1986, was second in the world cross-country championships in 1987, second in the Olympic 10,000m in 1988 and second in the world indoor 3000m in 1989. Having conquered the 10,000m world field in Tokyo, she went to New York to try a marathon. She won, first time out.

400-metre relay magic

WHATEVER it is that makes good relay runners, Britain seems to have it. Having won the 4 x 400m in the European championships of both 1986 and 1990, the lads did it again this year in both the European Cup and the world championships. For British eyes, there could hardly have been a more joyful spectacle than that of Kriss Akabusi overhauling the world individual champion, Pettigrew, to break the tape. Amazingly, three of that team of four (Black, Redmond, Regis and Akabusi) were in the winning team five years earlier.

Carling cuts through to the top of rugby

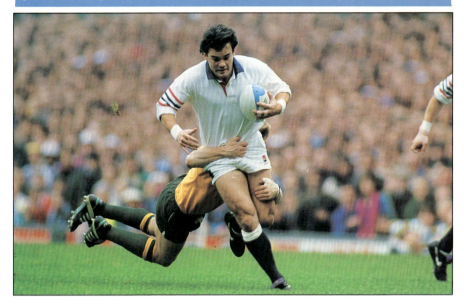

WILL CARLING, a startlingly young rugby captain of England, triumphantly vindicated the selectors' decision when he led his troops to two successive Grand Slams (1991 and 1992) and to the final of the World Cup at Twickenham. When he was appointed, some wondered whether he was even one of the best two centres in the land; by the time the World Cup was over many were rating him the best centre in the world.

Sidecar supremo strikes again

STEVE WEBSTER would pass as an unknown before most eyes, but he won the world sidecar championship in four of the past five years. In the altogether alarming world of motorcycle racing, this is the most hair-raising event, particularly for the passenger. Webster is the driver.

CHAMPIONS OF THE WORLD

Angling
Fly - Brian Leadbetter
Freshwater - Robert Nudd
Freshwater, team - Great Britain

Athletics
4 x 400m relay - United Kingdom
10,000m, women - Liz McColgan

Billiards
Mike Russell

Bowls
Indoor - Richard Corsie
Indoor, women - Mary Price

Boxing
Bantamweight - Duke McKenzie (WBO)

Canoeing
Slalom K1 - Shaun Pearce

Croquet
John Walters

Curling
Team - Scotland

Darts
Dennis Priestley

Hang Gliding
Team - Great Britain
Women - Judy Leden

Ice Skating
Speed, short track - Wilfred O'Reilly

Motor Cycling
Sidecar - Steve Webster

Motor Racing
Kart, 250cc - Martin Hines

Paragliding
Robbie Whittall

Powerlifting
44kg, women - Helen Wolsey

Rowing
Coxless pairs - Matthew Pinsent and Steven Redgrave
Coxless fours, lightweight - Great Britain

Shooting
Double trap - Peter Boden

Snooker
John Parrott

Squash
Team, women - England

WORLD RECORDS

Athletics
Relay, 4 x 200m - United Kingdom: 1min 22.11sec.
50km walk, women - Sandra Brown: 4hr 50min 51sec.

FOUNDATION FOR SPORT AND THE ARTS

THE Foundation for Sport and the Arts has existed since July 30th 1991. Established as a discretionary trust, it is anxious to work closely with existing organisations such as the national governing bodies of sport. Tim Rice is its Chairman and the other Trustees include Sir Richard Attenborough, Dame Janet Baker, Christopher Chataway, Richard Eyre and Clive Lloyd.

The Trust is funded by a contributory element provided for in the remittances of football pool clients, sent with their coupons. A third of the amount was made possible by a reduction in the rate of pool betting duty, agreed by Government on the basis that the Pool Promoters would arrange for the remainder.

Roughly two-thirds of its revenue (approaching £45m a year) is to be used for the benefit of sport and one-third for the arts. The philosphy of the Foundation is to reinforce what is already happening, to increase the use of existing facilities, to modernise current buildings or where appropriate construct new, and to assist projects that are already underway. The Foundation hopes to encourage outstanding initiative, enterprise and creativity. It is strongly desired that there should be substantial support for local activities in such a way that funds are fed into sport and the arts at community level. There is also scope for attention to major initiatives and the pursuit of excellence.

The Foundation seeks not to duplicate the efforts of other funding bodies. The criteria by which it operates are kept simple and the aim is to avoid fuss and bureaucracy.

Foundation for sport and the arts

COMMONWEALTH GAMES CHAMPIONS

1954
Athletics
880yd - D. Johnson
1 mile - R. Bannister
3 miles - C.J. Chataway
6 miles - P. Driver
Marathon - J. McGhee
4 x 440yd - England
Long jump - K. Wilmshurst
Pole vault - G. Elliott
Shot - J. Savidge
Triple jump - K. Wilmshurst
High jump, women - T Hopkins
Bowls
Pairs - W.J. Rosbotham and P.T. Watson
Boxing
Heavyweight - B. Harper
Welterweight - N Gargano
Bantamweight - J Smillie
Flyweight - R Currie
Cycling
Sprint - C.F. Peacock
Pursuit - N. Sheil
Road - E. Thompson
Diving
Springboard - P. Heatly
Springboard, women - A. Long
Fencing
Foil - Rene Paul
Sabre - M.J. Amberg
Epee, team - England
Foil, team - England
Foil, women - M. Glen Haig
Swimming
110yd backstroke - J. Brockway
220yd breaststroke, women - E. Gordon
3 x 110yd medley relay, women - Scotland
Weightlifting
75kg - J. Halliday
56kg - M. Megennis
Wrestling
Heavyweight - K. Richmond

1958
Athletics
4 x 110yd relay - England
Hammer - M. Ellis
Javelin - C. Smith
Pole vault - G. Elliott
Shot - A. Rowe
4 x 110yd relay, women - England
Discus, women - S. Allday
Long jump, women - S. Hoskin
Bowls
Fours - England
Boxing
Middleweight - T. Milligan
Lightweight - R. McTaggart
Bantamweight - H. Winstone
Flyweight - J. Brown
Cycling
Time trial - N. Tong
Pursuit - N. Sheil
Road - R. Booty
Diving
Highboard - P. Heatly
Springboard - K. Collin
Highboard, women - C. Welsh
Springboard, women - C. Welsh

Fencing
Epee - W. Hoskyns
Foil - Raymond Paul
Sabre - W. Hoskyns
Epee, team - England
Foil, team - England
Sabre, team - England
Foil, women - G. Sheen
Rowing
Double sculls - M. Spracklen and G. Baker
Coxless fours - England
Coxed fours - England
Swimming
220yd butterfly - I.M. Black
110yd backstroke, women - J. Grinham
220yd breaststroke - A. Lonsbrough
4 x 110yd medley relay, women - England
Weightlifting
110kg - K. MacDonald
82.5kg - P. Caira

1962
Athletics
Marathon - B. Kilby
4 x 110yd relay - England
Hammer - H. Payne
Shot - M. Lucking
100yd, women - D. Hyman
220yd, women - D. Hyman
Javelin, women - S. Platt
Bowls
Singles - D. Bryant
Fours - England
Boxing
Featherweight - J. McDermott
Flyweight - R. Mallon
Cycling
Road - W. Mason
Diving
Highboard - B. Phelps
Springboard - B. Phelps
Fencing
Foil - A. Leckie
Sabre - R. Cooperman
Epee, team - England
Foil, team - England
Sabre, team - England
Rowing
Double sculls - G. Justicz and N. Birkmyre
Pairs - S. Farquharson and J. Lee-Nicholson
Coxless fours - England
Swimming
110yd backstroke - G. Sykes
110yd backstroke, women - L. Ludgrove
220yd backstroke, women - L. Ludgrove
110yd breaststroke, women - A. Lonsbrough
220yd breaststroke, women - A. Lonsbrough
440yd individual medley, women - A. Lonsbrough

Weightlifting
90kg - L. Martin
82.5kg - P. Caira
67.5kg - C. Goring
60kg - G. Newton

1966
Athletics
Marathon - J. Alder
120yd hurdles - D. Hemery
20 mile walk - R. Wallwork
Hammer - H. Payne
Javelin - J. Fitzsimons
Long jump - L. Davies
Long jump, women - M. Rand
Badminton
Singles, women - A. Bairstow
Doubles, women - H. Horton and U. Smith
Doubles, mixed - R. Mills and A. Bairstow
Boxing
Light-heavyweight - R. Tighe
Light-middleweight - M. Rowe
Light-welterweight - J. McCourt
Cycling
Pursuit - H. Porter
10 miles - I. Alsop
Road - P. Buckley
Diving
Highboard - B. Phelps
Springboard - B. Phelps
Highboard, women - J. Newman
Springboard, women - K. Rowlatt
Fencing
Epee - W. Hoskyns
Foil - A. Jay
Sabre - R. Cooperman
Foil, women - J. Wardell-Yerburgh
Epee, team - England
Foil, team - England
Sabre, team - England
Foil, women's team - England
Shooting
Rifle, .303 - J. Swansea
Pistol, .22 - C. Sexton
Pistol, rapid fire - A. Clark
Swimming
110yd backstroke, women - L. Ludgrove
220yd backstroke, women - L. Ludgrove
110yd breaststroke, women - D. Harris
220yd breaststroke, women - J. Slattery
4 x 110yd medley relay, women - England
Weightlifting
90kg - L. Martin
60kg - K.W. Chung
56kg - P. McKenzie

1970
Athletics
5000m - I. Stewart
10,000m - L. Stewart
Marathon - R. Hill
110m hurdles - D. Hemery
400m hurdles - J. Sherwood
Hammer - H. Payne
Javelin - D. Travis
Long jump - L. Davies
Pole vault - M. Bull
800m, women - R. Stirling
1500m, women - R. Ridley
Discus, women - R. Payne
Long jump - S. Sherwood
Pentathlon - M. Peters
Shot - M. Peters
Badminton
Singles, women - M. Beck
Doubles, women - M. Boxall and S. Whetnall
Doubles, mixed - D. Talbot and M. Boxall
Bowls
Singles - D. Bryant
Pairs - N. King and P. Line
Boxing
Middleweight - J. Conteh
Light-middleweight - T. Imrie
Flyweight - D. Needham
Cycling
Pursuit - I. Hallam
Fencing
Epee - W. Hoskyns
Foil - M. Breckin
Sabre - A.M. Leckie
Foil, women - J. Wardell-Yerburgh
Epee, team - England
Foil, team - England
Sabre, team - England
Foil, women's team - England
Swimming
200m backstroke - M. Richards
100m butterfly, women - D. Langsley
Weightlifting
90kg - L. Martin
67.5kg - G. Newton
60kg - G. Perrin
56kg - P. McKenzie

1974
Athletics
Marathon - I. Thompson
400m hurdles - A. Pascoe
20 mile walk - J. Warhurst
Decathlon - M. Bull
Hammer - I. Chipchase
Javelin - C. Clover
Long jump - A. Lerwill
Shot - G. Capes
100m hurdles, women - J. Vernon
4 x 400m relay, women - England
High jump, women - B. Lawton
Pentathlon - M. Peters
Badminton
Doubles - D. Talbot and E. Stuart
Singles, women - G. Gilks
Doubles, women - M. Beck and G. Gilks
Doubles, mixed - D. Talbot and G. Gilks

Bowls
Singles - D. Bryant
Pairs - J. Christie and A. McIntosh
Boxing
Heavyweight - N. Meade
Light-heavyweight - W. Knight
Bantamweight - P. Cowdell
Flyweight - D. Larmour
Cycling
Pursuit - I. Hallam
10 mile - S. Heffernan
Tandem sprint - G. Cooke and E. Crutchlow
Team pursuit - England
Swimming
100m breaststroke - D. Leigh
200m breaststroke - D. Wilkie
200m butterfly - B. Brinkley
200m medley - D. Wilkie
100m breaststroke, women - C. Gaskell
200m breaststroke, women - P. Beavan
Weightlifting
82.5kg - T. Ford
67.5kg - G. Newton
52kg - P. McKenzie

1978
Athletics
200m - A. Wells
1500m - D. Moorcroft
10,000m - B. Foster
110m hurdles - B. Price
4 x 100m relay - Scotland
30km walk - O. Flynn
Decathlon - D. Thompson
Long jump - R. Mitchell
Triple jump - K. Connor
Shot - G. Capes
100m, women - S. Lannaman
400m, women - D. Hartley
1500m, women - M. Stewart
3000m, women - P. Fudge
100m hurdles - L. Boothe
4 x 100m relay, women - England
4 x 400m relay, women - England
Javelin, women - T. Sanderson
Long jump, women - S. Reeve
Badminton
Doubles - R. Stevens and M. Tredgett
Doubles, women - N. Perry and A. Statt
Doubles, mixed - M. Tredgett and N. Perry
Team - England
Bowls
Singles - D. Bryant
Boxing
Heavyweight - J. Awome
Lightweight - G. Hamil
Bantamweight - B. McGuigan
Diving
Highboard - C. Snode
Springboard - C. Snode
Shooting
Rifle, .22 - A. Allan
Swimming
200m medley, women - S. Davies
400m medley, women - S. Davies
Weightlifting
90kg - G. Langford

1982
Athletics
100m - A. Wells
200m - M. McFarlane and A. Wells
1500m - S. Cram
5000m - D. Moorcroft
4 x 400m relay - England
30km walk - S. Barry
Decathlon - D. Thompson
Hammer - R. Weir
Triple jump - K. Connor
800m, women - K. McDermott
1500m, women - C. Boxer
100m hurdles, women - S. Strong
4 x 100m relay, women - England
Discus, women - M. Ritchie
Shot, women - J. Oakes
Badminton
Singles, women - H. Troke
Doubles, mixed - M. Dew and K. Chapman
Team - England
Bowls
Singles - W. Wood
Pairs - D. Gourlay and J. Watson
Boxing
Middleweight - J. Price
Welterweight - C. Pyatt
Cycling
Road - M. Elliott
Team time trial - England
Diving
Highboard - C. Snode
Springboard - C. Snode
Shooting
Rifle, .22 prone, pairs - M. Cooper and M. Sullivan
Rifle, .22 3-position - A. Allan
Rifle, .22 3-position, pairs - M. Cooper and B. Dagger
Rifle, full bore - A. Clarke
Pistol, centre fire - J. Cooke
Air pistol - G. Darling
Air rifle, pairs - A. Allan and B. McNeil
Olympic trap - P. Boden
Swimming
200m freestyle - A. Astbury
400m freestyle - A. Astbury
100m breaststroke - A. Moorhouse
200m butterfly - P. Hubble
100m freestyle, women - J. Croft
200m freestyle, women - J. Croft
4 x 100m freestyle relay, women - England
Weightlifting
110kg - J. Burns
82.5kg - N. Burrowes
75kg - S. Pinsent
67.5kg - D. Morgan
60kg - D. Willey
56kg - D. Laws
Wrestling
Bantamweight - B. Aspen

1986
Athletics
400m - R. Black
800m - S. Cram
1500m - S. Cram
5000m - S. Ovett
10,000m - J. Solly
400m hurdles - P. Beattie
4 x 400m relay - England
Decathlon - D. Thompson
Hammer - D. Smith
Javelin - D. Ottley
Pole vault - A. Ashurst
Shot - B. Cole
Triple jump - J. Herbert
100m, women - H. Oakes
800m women - K. Wade
1500m - K. Wade
10,000m - E. Lynch
100m hurdles - S. Gunnell
4 x 100m relay, women - England
Heptathlon - J. Simpson
Javelin - T. Sanderson
Long jump - J. Oladapo
Badminton
Singles - S. Baddeley
Doubles - W. Gilliland and D. Travers
Singles, women - H. Troke
Doubles, women - G. Clark and G. Gowers
Team - England
Bowls
Pairs - G. Adrain and G. Knox
Fours - Wales
Singles, women - W. Line
Pairs, women - N.Ireland
Fours, women - Wales
Boxing
Light-heavyweight - J. Moran
Middleweight - R. Douglas
Welterweight - D. Dyer
Bantamweight - S. Murphy
Flyweight - J. Lyon
Cycling
Team time trial - England
Road - P. Curran
Rowing
Single sculls - S. Redgrave
Coxless pairs - S. Redgrave and A. Holmes
Coxed fours - England
Coxless fours, lightweight - England
Coxless fours, lightweight, women - England
Shooting
Rifle, .22 3-position - M. Cooper
Rifle, .22 3-position, pairs - M. Cooper and S. Cooper
Pistol, centre fire - R. Northover
Pistol, rapid fire, pairs - B. Girling and T. Turner
Air pistol, pairs - P. Leatherdale and I. Reid
Olympic trap - I. Peel
Olympic trap, pairs - P. Boden and I. Peel
Skeet - N. Kelly
Skeet, pairs - K. Harman and J. Neville
Swimming
200m breaststroke - A. Moorhouse
100m butterfly - A. Jameson
400m freestyle, women - S. Hardcastle
800m freestyle, women - S. Hardcastle
100m butterfly, women - C. Cooper
4 x 100m medley relay, women - England
Weightlifting
90kg - K. Boxell
82.5kg - D. Morgan
67.5kg - D. Willey
60kg - R. Williams
Wrestling
Light-heavyweight - N. Loban

1990
Athletics
100m - L. Christie
200m - M. Adam
1500m - P. Elliott
10,000m - E. Martin
110m hurdles - C. Jackson
400m hurdles - K. Akabusi
4 x 100m relay - England
Javelin - S. Backley
Shot - S. Williams
800m, women - D. Edwards
10,000m, women - E. McColgan
100m hurdles, women - K. Morley
400m hurdles, women - S. Gunnell
4 x 400m relay, women - England
Javelin - T. Sanderson
Shot, women - M. Augee
Badminton
Singles, women - F. Smith
Doubles, women - F. Smith and S. Sankey
Team - England
Bowls
Fours - Scotland
Boxing
Light-middleweight - R. Woodhall
Light-welterweight - C. Kane
Featherweight - J. Irkwin
Cycling
Sprint, women - L. Jones
Diving
Highboard - R. Morgan
Judo
Open - E. Gordon
95+kg - E. Gordon
95kg - R. Stevens
86kg - D. White
78kg - D. Southby
71kg - R. Stone
60kg - C. Finney
Open, women - S. Lee
72+kg, women - S. Lee
72kg, women - J. Morris
66kg, women - S. Mills
61kg, women - D. Bell
56kg, women - L. Cusack
52kg, women - S. Rendle
48kg, women - K. Briggs
Shooting
Full bore - C. Mallett
Full bore, pairs - S. Belither and A. Tucker
Pistol, rapid fire - A. Breton
Olympic trap, pairs - K. Gill and I. Peel
Skeet - K. Harman
Skeet, pairs - J. Dunlop and I. Marsden
Swimming
100m breaststroke - A. Moorhouse
Weightlifting
110+kg - A. Davies
110kg - M. Thomas
100kg - A. Saxton
90kg - D. Dawkins
82.5kg - D. Morgan

EUROPEAN ATHLETICS CHAMPIONS

1954
1500m - R. Bannister
High jump, women - T. Hopkins
Long jump, women - J. Desforges

1958
400m - J. Wrighton
800m - M. Rawson
1500m - B. Hewson
20km walk - S. Vickers
4 x 100m relay - United Kingdom
4 x 400m relay - United Kingdom
Shot - A. Rowe
4 x 100m relay, women - United Kingdom

1962
400m - R. Brightwell
5000m - B. Tulloh
Marathon - B. Kilby
20km walk - K. Matthews
100m, women - D. Hyman
200m, women - D. Hyman

1966
Long jump - L. Davies

1969
1500m - J. Whetton
5000m - I. Stewart
Marathon - R. Hill
20km walk - P. Nihill
4 x 400m relay, women - United Kingdom

1974
Marathon - I. Thompson
400m hurdles - A. Pascoe

1982
1500m - S. Cram
Decathlon - D. Thompson
Triple jump - K. Connor

1986
100m - L. Christie
400m - R. Black
800m - S. Coe
1500m - S. Cram
5000m - J. Buckner
4 x 400m relay - United Kingdom
Decathlon - D. Thompson
Javelin, women - F. Whitbread

1990
200m - J. Regis
400m - R. Black
800m - T. McKean
4 x 400m relay - United Kingdom
110m hurdles - C. Jackson
400m hurdles - K. Akabusi
Javelin - S. Backley
3000m, women - Y. Murray

OTHER SPORTS, OTHER BRITISH CHAMPIONS

Archery
European Champion
Field:
B.Fielding (1971).

Ballroom Dancing
World Champions
Latin:
L.Patrick and D.Kay (1959),
B.Irvine and R.Irvine (1961-66-68),
W.Laird and Lorraine (1962-3-4),
A.Hurley and F.Saxton (1972),
P.Maxwell and L.Harman (1976),
A.Fletcher and H.Fletcher (1977-78-79-80-81),
D.Burns and G.Fairweather (1984-85-86-87-88-89-90-91).
Modern:
D.Ellison and B.Winslade (1959),
B.Irvine and R.Irvine (1960-62-63-64-65-67-68),
H.Smith-Hampshire and D.Gray (1961),
P.Eggleton and B.Winslade (1966-69-70),
A.Hurley and F.Saxton (1971),
R.Gleave and J.Gleave (1973-74-75-76-77-78-79),
M.Barr and V.Barr (1980-81-82-83-84-85),
S.Hillier and L.Hillier (1986-87-88),
J.Wood and A.Lewis (1989).
Ten-dance:
P.Eggleton and D.Gradwell (1959),
D.Sycamore and D.Weavers (1980-81-82-83-84-85),
M.Hilton and K.Hilton (1986-90-91).
Latin, amateur:
R.Taylor and A.Gent (1964),
J.Wesley and B.Wesley (1965),
R.Root and F.Spires (1969),
A.Fletcher and H.Fletcher (1972-73),
P.Maxwell and L.Harman (1974),
J.Walker and R.Walker (1975),
J.Robinson and D.London (1977),
D.Sycamore and D.Weavers (1978-79),
D.Burns and G.Fairweather (1981),
M.Hilton and K.Johnstone (1982-83).
Latin team, amateur:
Penge (1965-67-68-69).

Modern, amateur:
M.Houseman and V.Waite (1960),
A.Hurley and F.Saxton (1961),
L.Armstrong and E.Welch (1962),
J.Wesley and B.Wesley (1963-64-65),
G.Coad and P.Thompson (1966-67),
M.Higgins and J.Hunt (1968),
R.Gleave and J.Wade (1969-70),
B.Charlton and M.Alexander (1971),
M.Barr and V.Green (1972-73),
F.Venables and L.Horwood (1974),
G.Boyce and L.Boyce (1975),
R.Grover and B.Grover (1976),
S.Hillier and L.Tate (1978),
K.Welsh and K.Gilmartin (1981),
J.Wood and H.Stuart (1983),
A.Sinkinson and L.Barry (1988-89).
Ten-dance, amateur:
M.Houseman and V.Waite (1960),
J.Wesley and B.Wesley (1963),
M.Hilton and K.Johnstone (1982).

Bridge
World Champions
Olympiad pairs, women:
R.Markus (1962-74),
J.Durran and J.Juan (1966)
Olympiad team, women:
Great Britain (1964)
Team, women (Venice Trophy):
Great Britain (1981-85).
Team, men:
Great Britain (1955).
European Champions
Team, men:
Great Britain (1954-61-63-91)
Team, women:
Great Britain (1952-59-61-63-66-75-79-81).

Golf
The Open:
T.Jacklin (1969),
S.Lyle (1985),
N.Faldo (1987-90).
US Open:
T.Jacklin (1970).
US Masters:
S.Lyle (1988),
N.Faldo (1989-90),
I.Woosnam (1991).

Ryder Cup:
Great Britain (1957),
Europe (1985-87).
World Cup:
D.Llewelyn and I.Woosnam (Wales) (1987).

Horse Racing
Champion Jockeys
Flat:
G.Richards (1952-53),
D.Smith (1954-55-56-58-59),
S.Breasley (1957-61-62-63),
L.Piggott (1960-64-65-66-67-68-69-70-71-81-82),
W.Carson (1972-73-78-80-83),
P.Eddery (1974-75-76-77-86-88-89-90),
J.Mercer (1979),
S.Cauthen (1984-85-87).
National Hunt:
T.Molony (1952-55),
F.Winter (1953-56-57-58),
R.Francis (1954),
T.Brookshaw (1959),
S.Mellor (1960-61-62),
J.Gifford (1963-64-67-68),
T.Biddlecombe (1965-66-69),
R.Davies (1969-70-72),
G.Thorner (1971),
R.Barry (1973-74),
T.Stack (1975-77),
J.Francome (1976-79-81-82-83-84-85),
J.O'Neill (1978-80),
P.Scudamore (1982-86-87-88-89-90-91-92).

Ice Skating
European Champions
Figure skating:
J.Altwegg (1952),
J.Nicks and J.Nicks (pairs, 1963),
J.Curry (1976),
R.Cousins (1980).
Ice dance:
L.Demmy and J.Westwood (1954-55),
P.Thomas and P.Weight (1956),
C.Jones and J.Markham (1957-58),
C.Jones and D.Denny (1959-60-61),
B.Ford and D.Towler (1968),
C.Dean and J.Torvill (1981-82-84).

Rugby Union
Grand Slams:
Wales (1952-71-76-78),
England (1957-80-91-92),
Scotland (1984-90).

Sea Angling
World Champions
Boat:
J.Pressley (1991).
Boat team:
England (1991).
Conger:
R.Page (1962).
Shore team:
England (1990).
European Champions
Boat:
M.North (1974).
Tope:
J.Reece (1973-74-75).

Tennis
Wimbledon: Women
A.Mortimer (1961),
A.Jones (1969),
V.Wade (1977).
United States: Women
V.Wade (1968).
France: Women
A.Mortimer (1955),
S.Bloomer (1957),
C.Truman (1959),
A.Haydon/Jones (1961-66),
S.Barker (1976).
Australia: Women
A.Mortimer (1958),
V.Wade (1972).

Weightlifting
European Champions
90kg - L.Martin (1959-62-63-65).
82.5kg, women - J.Oakes (1989-90).
67.5kg, women - J.Rose (1991).
56kg, women - M.Forteath (1988).
52kg, women - P.Haughton (1988).

Britain's 342 world and Olympic champions are listed at the beginning of the book. These winners of other international contests are a sample of the rich variety of our Champions of the Queen.